SOUTHERN APPETIZERS

SOUTHERN
APPETIZERS

60 Delectables for Gracious Get-Togethers

DENISE GEE

PHOTOGRAPHS BY ROBERT M. PEACOCK

CHRONICLE BOOKS

SAN FRANCISCO

For Evelyn Dauphin, the life of every party, for teaching
me how to be a good listener. And to wear red lipstick.

Library of Congress Cataloging-in-Publication Data available.
ISBN: 978-1-4521-3296-9

Manufactured in China

FSC
www.fsc.org

MIX
Paper from
responsible sources
FSC™ C008047

Designed by Stitch Design Co.
Food and prop styling by Denise Gee

10 9 8 7 6 5 4 3 2 1

Chronicle Books LLC
680 Second Street
San Francisco, California 94107
www.chroniclebooks.com

Permissions

Page 31: Emeril's Tomato Jam used with permission from
Chef Emeril Lagasse.

Page 60: Oysters Rockefeller Spinach Dip adapted from *The
Cooking Club Cookbook* (Villard) with permission from author
Katherine Fausset and Random House.

Page 115: Pascal's Manale BBQ Shrimp adapted from a recipe
shared by New Orleans restaurant Pascal's Manale, used with
their permission.

Page 116: Dickie Brennan's Oyster Pan Roast used with
permission from Chef Dickie Brennan of The Palace Café in
New Orleans.

Page 126: Stanley's Juleps used with permission from author
Stanley Dry.

Contents

Introduction

Watch closely. At just about any party down South, it's uncanny how arriving party guests, wearing broad smiles, peer right past the welcoming host to zero in on their intended target: the appetizer table. A hostess would be kidding herself to think the evening's true mission would involve bonding over deep, meaningful conversation. Nope, it's all about the food. And often the booze, but always the food. I'm a victim of that way of thinking myself. Just watch as I sashay first and foremost to the feeding line. Oysters Rockefeller dip trumps small talk on any day, and makes a party ripe for lingering. But dry, bland sausage balls? Or water chestnuts wrapped in nearly raw bacon? You can bet that after a bit of banter, guests will be scampering home early.

The recipes selected for a Southern party mean way more than any luxury vehicle or infinity pool the host may have prominently on display. Party foods are the keys to the social kingdom, and they'll make or break you. Too little food? Busted. Too little flavor? Not good. But if you play your cards right, which I aim to help you do, having the right mix of appetizers can transform you into a god or goddess. (Especially with help from soft lighting and dark clothing, and something bright and shiny up near the face, but I digress.)

Understanding the importance of offering the right mix of food (see the recipes that follow) and the right mix of people (you're on your own) seems to come with Southern birthing papers. That's particularly true for my family, which loves to entertain.

Consider my hometown of Natchez, Mississippi, a river-city cousin to New Orleans, some three hours south.

At any given party, being the first to wield the heftiest appetizer plate was often the order of the day. "Excuse me, I didn't see you, I was so busy talking," a well-fed socialite might say to the person in front of her who, in an instant, had become the person behind her. "Now, tell me, honey, who you are. You look *so* familiar. My, doesn't *this* look good. . . . "

Competition is fierce at such soirees, but it's always washed down in a honey-sweet way that makes you somehow feel privileged to give up your hard-won spot in line. With her plate near-listing from so much food, Mrs. Somethingorother would lament not having room for anything else. "Do let me know how those shrimp thingys are. I might have to come back. I'm just about to *die* of hunger." And off she'd float to some remote spot, joining some other kindred spirit wanting to eat well, but discreetly. "Oh, do come and join me," Mrs. Somethingorother's well-coiffed counterpart might sheepishly say, acknowledging the heft on her plate. "I haven't eaten *a thing* all day."

Back at the buffet table, people can be found circling, with steely yet congenial resolve, to partake of myriad dips, spreads, puffs, tarts, biscuits, and carved meats served on or in the grandest of silver dishes and heirloom china casseroles.

Though these days I rarely see such over-the-top grandeur, the intent to impress lives on.

The idea to put in print the South's best appetizers occurred to me while paging through a tattered collection of recipe binders I keep in the kitchen. The appetizer volume, plump and haggard, appears the most cherished of them all, brimming with recipes from my family, my imagination, or party hosts I hounded after momentous dining occasions. I noticed that many of the recipes had been typed and re-typed, copied and re-copied, for people who, like me, realized they couldn't live without them.

The thing is, we unabashedly adore appetizers in the South. Often they're the only things we order off of restaurant menus. And rarely do we have proper sit-down dinners anymore. It's all about keeping your options open. At a cocktail party, the focus will forever be on the appetizers—smoked pecans on the sideboard, cheese straws on the coffee table, an array of hot dips in the dining room, and pickled shrimp on the porch. A labyrinth that doesn't just inspire you to mingle, it forces you to do so. And nowadays, there's less shame in eating to your heart's desire. In fact, we live for it.

A Mississippi chef friend once told me that while living in the Midwest, she realized she'd taken for granted that Southerners will gather for food and drinks at the drop of a hat. To wit: Wanting to break the ice with a buttoned-up group planning to attend an opera event, she invited them to stop by her home for a few appetizers and cocktails. "You mean, food and drinks *before* the show?" an invitee inquired. "They'll have food and drinks in the lobby. Why bother?"

Good heavens! Why bother? We're not pretzel people, darling. And we haven't had *a thing* to eat all day.

CHAPTER ONE

DETAILS, DETAILS:

Prepping for the Party

Since the dawning of the hushpuppy—the original "small bite"—Southerners have been enamored with nibbles. As for why, I can think of two reasons.

The South's strong cocktail culture has long made it de rigueur for those with a fondness for drinking to eat dinner only after a cocktail "hour" (or two or three). And since appetizers don't technically count as dinner, hors d'oeuvres delightfully extend drinking sessions.

Furthermore, the best events were, and continue to be, "heavy appetizer" cocktail parties, where guests can imbibe unfettered while wandering room to room, trying a little of this and that, Whitman's Sampler–style.

As we carry forth this tradition, know this much is true: Bountiful Southern nibbles, barrels of liquid refreshment, a charming décor and comfy setting, a breezy style and fun group of people—if you build it, they will come. Count on it.

GET PLANNING

The secrets to throwing a good party are (1) over-prepare and then go with the flow and (2) don't let on that you've done any such thing. The trick is to create the illusion of effortless elegance.

While some of the best gatherings are impromptu, the real winners are ones for which the host has done his or her homework, knowing full well that good planning lets everyone (host included) enjoy the party. And a major part of any party's success is what's served—the food and beverages.

The appetizers in this book aren't meant to be enjoyed only at parties, per se; all of them can be savored at home before a family meal. But how nice it is to gather them, like good friends, and collectively use them to pamper your guests with delicious hospitality.

I'm a fan of buffet-style appetizer parties. They offer more freedom and less fuss, which works nicely for open house–style gatherings. The drop-by-when-you-can mindset takes the pressure off people to be at a certain place at a certain time for an extended period. On the contrary, open-house fêtes allow people to swing by when convenient. When they do arrive, their relaxed vibe is not only a positive influence on others, but it also keeps the party conversation fluid and lively.

For help in making the party plan go even more smoothly, ask family members and friends to monitor specific aspects—such as keeping the food hot, checking the beverage station, and greeting new arrivals. (And for advice on serving party fare for these occasions, see "Organizing the Buffet" on page 14.)

For a grander, more formal party, especially a large one, do not, under any circumstance, try to handle it yourself. Frazzled hosts beget frazzled guests, and bring any chance of a relaxing setting to a thud. Support fellow foodies by hiring a good caterer, one whose food you've admired elsewhere or one recommended by a trusted friend.

Here are a few basic guidelines to consider while planning:

- For an hors d'oeuvres–only party, plan on five to eight appetizers. If the starters are only meant to tide people over before dinner, go with, say, three light choices, one of which can include nuts.

- If guests mostly will be standing, drink in hand, offer one- or two-bite foods that can be passed around on pretty platters (served with paper napkins for dabbing fingers and mouths) or easily accessible on serving tables.

- If any appetizer needs a utensil or two, or requires a bit of concentration to not make a mess, ensure everyone has a place to sit to eat it.

- Make more food and garnish ingredients than you'll need. If you're expecting fifteen guests, have enough for twenty-four people. That not only will accommodate unexpected visitors, but also will allow you to replenish food that begins to look bedraggled.

- Balance offerings when possible. If there's something salty (like Muffaletta Bites, page 28), there might also be something sweet (like Minted Watermelon & Feta Salad, page 88). If something's creamy (like Shrimp Butter, page 74), there should also be something crunchy (like Fanciful Cheese Straws, page 20). For something spicy (such as Lil' Natchitoches Meat Pies, page 44), have something cooling (such as Goodly Ranch Dip, page 58). For something traditional (such as Just-Right Cocktail Pecans, page 23), serve something a bit more modern (such as Strawberry-Beet Salsa, page 73).

- Take it easier. Plan for some dishes to be bought ahead of time (e.g., restaurant-quality tortilla chips) and others that can be made a day or so in advance (like dips).

- For ideas on party themes and food that fills the bill, see "Party Themes & Menus" on page 136.

Catering Pointers

One-size-fits-all catering can yield dated or ho-hum food; don't feel like you can't have input into what you'll serve. Hopefully the person you plan to hire is a good listener who'll understand your tastes and help you make a meaningful impression on your guests. And if you know you'd like an oysters Rockefeller dip or exquisite sauce for shrimp cocktail, by all means share recipes from this book or other favorites.

If your catered event will have an open bar, don't let the catering staff talk you into paying more for them to provide a bartender, a.k.a. one of the catering support crew (likely to arrive with a drink guide in tow). Unless you can verify that person's bartending skills, check with a respected restaurant bartender and ask if he or she can be hired away for the event (something that can even be promoted on the invite) or knows of a good drink mixer.

Inviting Notions

Impress upon your guests how fun the party will be by sending them a cleverly designed invitation on high-quality paper stock. Why send snail-mail in the digital age? Picture your computer's "in" box. See it overrun by junk mail. Recall the paltry amount of printed mail you receive. Realize, then, that a hand-addressed or personalized card is truly a delight to behold.

The vast expanse of the World Wide Web works to our advantage in that it offers a world of opportunities to find creative graphic artists' work.

As a general rule, send invitations three or four weeks before your event, asking for guests to RSVP seven to ten days beforehand.

Invites also can include a note asking guests to advise you of any significant dietary restrictions or allergies.

SETTING THE SCENE

With much to be said and done about party décor, the main thing is to ensure there'll be enough space for everyone to mix and mingle with ease. You'll want to enlist every space you can for intimate sitting areas. You'll also want plenty of side tables (accent pieces, small benches, ceramic stools), since there's nothing worse than not having any place to put a drink or plate. (Which reminds me, coasters, coasters, coasters. They should be everywhere, especially if you have wood furniture. Little bread plates work nicely, too.)

For overall décor, consider the bridal adage "something old, something new, something borrowed, and something blue"—but in lieu of "blue" let's make it "hue."

- **Something old:** A special piece of furniture, table linen, or set of dishes you've inherited or collected make nice conversation pieces. One of my favorite ideas is using old (washable) quilts or chenille bedspreads atop outdoor tables. While burlap isn't old, it gives the patina of age, as do modern wares made of vintage-style galvanized metal. Hammered tin or etched aluminum serving pieces offer even more shiny (and affordable) bling.

- **Something new:** Now's the time to replace those faded, raggedy outdoor furniture cushions. While you're at it, add a stylish outdoor rug. They'll provide fresh, clean pops of color and help define inviting gathering spots.

- **Something borrowed:** Remember the porcelain baby bathtub on a stand your cousin found at the antiques fair? The one she used to ice down drinks? Ask to borrow it. (But do promise you'll keep a death grip on it, so to speak—that you'll return it in better shape than it was when you got it.) Rented items fall into this category too. Consider renting chairs and tables from party supply stores, which often will drop off and pick up items for free. Antiques shops will also sometimes rent unique furnishings for a 10- to 15-percent fee.

- **Something hue:** While "something blue" works for me because I adore it, I realize it doesn't go with everything. The main idea is to decide on a fitting color scheme and stick with it—carefully. Just like the menu's harmony of flavors and colors and textures, the same goes for decorating. Designers call it "color-blocking."

Take, for example, the Mardi Gras colors of gold/yellow, green, and purple. You have to admit it's a frightful combination, at least collectively, which means you'd want to avoid having gold, green, and purple flowers all in the same vase. The same goes for your overall décor. Though all the colors could fittingly festoon a door wreath, your party décor will benefit from keeping them in "blocks." For instance, the main serving or dining table could have a mix of yellow-gold flowers atop a neutral burlap. Plates could be white, maybe trimmed in gold, and topped with yellow-gold linen napkins. Green could be worked into the scheme by way of ivy topiaries or herbs tucked into the napkins. Small bursts of purple could come via a few beads snaking through candle votives or vases of irises or freesia used elsewhere.

Focal Point

• • •

Ensuring at least one of your table's glasses is colored and/or patterned not only will break up the visual monotony of a clear-glass expanse but also can help deter gesturers like me from potentially backhanding one of said glasses into oblivion.

Ideas in Bloom

Flowers and plants always look best natural and unfussy. Consider the following:

- Queen Anne's lace looks gorgeous in a white, cream, or transferware pitcher, as do hydrangea blossoms in a decorative tureen.

- For a more elegant arrangement, combine a dreamy mix of tone-on-tone heirloom-style flowers (say, tulips, dahlias, ranunculus, and hydrangeas).

- Small bouquets of tiny, shapely flowers look sweet in mercury glass votive holders atop dinner plates; they also can be gifts to your guests after your party.

- Gerberas or spider mums add festive, sculptural interest to vintage soft-drink bottles (and also can be given as gifts).

- Julep cups are even more refined when filled with heirloom roses.

- A large pot of fresh mint and/or rosemary near your front door provides an aromatic welcome for visitors (and makes a good source for cocktail or food garnishes).

Hydrangea Power
• • •

There are several tricks to prolonging the life of the South's beautiful pink, blue, or white "big leaf" or "French" hydrangea blooms. To prevent wilting (theirs and yours), follow these steps, using them in a vase or vessel.

- Heat a cup of water to near boiling. Place it next to a cup of cool water.

- Using a sharp knife, not scissors, slice each hydrangea stem at a sharp angle to give it the widest possible opening for all-important water absorption. (Dull scissors can "pinch" closed the stem base, lessening water intake.)

- Immediately after cutting each stem, place it in the hot water for 30 seconds before plunging it into the cool water for 15 to 20 seconds. Doing this will "force" good water absorption to help lessen the cut's impact.

- Place the cut stems in a presentation vessel, preferably fitted with water-soaked florist foam to help secure the blooms.

ORGANIZING THE BUFFET

A buffet can be an easy and elegant way to casually entertain if you follow a few simple suggestions:

- Use a long farm table, sideboard, or kitchen island/counter for the bulk of dishes. Place easier-to-eat dips and other such snacks on tables throughout the party. Keep beverage and dessert stations in other areas that won't create traffic jams or big problems in case of spills.

- Avoid the look of a potluck supper or church pie sale by varying the heights of food on tiered platters and stacked cake stands. Place other dishes, like baskets lined with tea towels and pretty platters, atop small, sturdy boxes or upside-down bowls covered in fabric. Keep sauces low so they won't drip on foods for which they're not intended.

- Arrange the buffet by having small plates (6- to 7-inch salad or dessert ones) at the start of the food flow, and rolled napkins (with utensils tucked inside, if needed) at the end of it. This way guests won't have to juggle much while negotiating various foods.

- Keep foods indoors to avoid attracting insects that will want in on the action. If you must have food outside, cover it with small mesh food tents, shoo-fly domes, or glass cake lids.

- Let guests know what they're about to eat (or not) by using small frames or cards identifying each dish.

Playing It Safe
• • •

Keep food meant to be cold on ice or don't leave it out for long—especially mayonnaise-based fare. As a general rule, food shouldn't sit out longer than two hours. And it should never sit in direct sunlight, which acts as a heat lamp. Also, make sure serving dishes are food-safe or oven-safe; that white bowl may look cool, but it may be for decorative purposes only.

Chafing Dish Primer

By design, chafing dishes (a buffet's best friend) keep party food hot via a specially designed dish that sits snugly in a pan of water within a raised frame. The bottom "steam" pan is heated by either cooking fuel (think Sterno), electricity, or a candle. Some handy tips include:

- Modern chafing dishes are geared to keep hot food hot—not heat it up; the food you'll be serving needs to be at the desired temperature *before* it's available for public consumption. Make sure the food's temperature stays above 140°F (otherwise bacteria might form) but below 160°F (or it will scorch).

- Ensure the water in a steam pan is at least $1\frac{1}{2}$ inches beneath the food. Check the level periodically and replenish as needed.

- Cooking fuel, a nontoxic and biodegradable mix of alcohol, water, and gel, burns for about 2 hours, which is the maximum length of time a dish of food should stay out anyway.

- Fuel canisters, available from hardware and party supply stores, can go into action once you remove the lid from the canister, slide it into the round space beneath the pan, and light the wick with a barbecue lighter.

- Keep a watchful eye on candles and canister flames. Once the latter burns out, let it cool before attempting to remove it. (Fortunately fuel canisters now have labels that let you know when they're safe to touch.)

- Newfangled chafing dishes run about $50, but vintage ones, often more decorative, can be half the cost (but don't offer temperature-control options or a water pan). New ones can often be rented from party supply stores.

- Keep the dish tightly covered to retain heat and moisture. Remove the lid carefully and slowly to avoid burning yourself.

- Stir the food occasionally to ensure it heats evenly (and looks its best).

FAST FIXES

For impromptu parties or last-minute potlucks, here's fare that can be pulled from the pantry, fridge, or freezer or purchased at a market or eatery:

- Baked cheese straws
- Boiled or roasted peanuts
- Fried chicken tenders and honey-mustard sauce
- Good pimiento cheese with cucumber slices, celery sections, or crackers
- Hummus with pita chips
- Pickled okra or green beans
- Queso, guacamole, salsa, and tortilla chips from a Mexican restaurant
- Seasoned popcorn or chips
- Small hot tamales
- "Slider" buns, chopped pork, coleslaw, and light BBQ sauce
- Spiced pecans, cashews, or almonds
- Spinach dip with hearty crackers
- Steamed, seasoned shrimp with cocktail or rémoulade sauce

10 Ways to Make It Snappy

When time's short but expectations are high, consider some easy ways to assuage your guests' appetites.

1. Fill mini phyllo shells with good-quality chicken salad (such as Curried Chicken Salad, page 49) and/or cream cheese blended with mango chutney; sprinkle with toasted, chopped pecans or sliced almonds.

2. Top crackers with cream cheese, hot-pepper jelly, and toasted pecan pieces.

3. Toast or fry breaded, parboiled ravioli and serve with marinara sauce.

4. Heat mini meatballs in thick, sweet BBQ sauce.

5. Marinate cooked cheese tortellini in Italian dressing.

6. Wrap chunks of cantaloupe or honeydew melon with prosciutto strips; secure with wooden picks and drizzle with lime juice or honey.

7. Layer slices of Roma tomatoes, fresh mozzarella or goat cheese, and basil leaves; flavor with olive oil and freshly ground salt and pepper.

8. Gently combine blue cheese or Gorgonzola crumbles with toasted pecan or walnut pieces; stuff into endive leaves and drizzle with light honey or agave syrup.

9. Add lemon or orange zest to marinated olives.

10. Mix sour cream with a flavorful seasoning blend for a quick dip; I love Cavender's, a Greek seasoning made in the unlikeliest of places—the Ozark Mountains (see Sources, page 138).

BARTENDING—
BY THE NUMBERS

This is helpful advice for deciding how many bottles and bags of ice you'll need for entertaining:

- Wine—One bottle equals 750 milliliters or 25 ounces, which yields five to six servings per bottle, depending on your pour (bartenders recommend planning on half a bottle per person).

- Beer—Assume guests will drink about 12 ounces (one bottle) of beer every half hour to hour during the party.

- Cocktails—Use $1\frac{1}{2}$ ounces of liquor for each drink.

- Liquor—A "fifth" bottle equals about 750 milliliters or 25 ounces, which yields about sixteen $1\frac{1}{2}$-ounce pours.

- Soda—One liter equals about 34 ounces, more than five 6-ounce servings.

- Ice—Plan for 2 pounds of ice per guest for drinks with ice, plus lots more cubed or crushed ice for chilling beer and wine. Fill coolers with ice if you don't have room in the freezer, but keep the coolers outside, since they have a tendency to leak water (and on occasion, need to be drained before adding more ice). For six guests, get 10 pounds of extra ice; twelve guests, 24 pounds.

- Glasses—Purchase or rent glasses or get your partyware out of storage. Whether you're using actual glass or plastic, expect guests to use multiples. For six guests, keep on hand 16 glasses; twelve guests, 30 glasses. Up those numbers when serving a variety of drinks (cocktails, wine, beer, apéritifs).

Pop Art
• • •

- Show guests both young and old how creative and thoughtful you are by offering a festive array of carbonated drinks—be they soft drinks, pops, sodas, or "Cokes" (the Southern catch-all word for any carbonated beverage).

- Use an ice scoop for drinks requiring ice but not for the ice that chills canned or bottled sodas and water. Don't use that ice for drinks since everyone's hands will have been in it, scoop or no scoop.

TWO FINAL TIPS FOR THE
SOUTHERN PARTY HOST

Pretty is as pretty does, my grandmother always said. That applies to the overall message of this book.

Think pretty—this is what I was trained to do while at the *Southern Living* charm school of magazine production twenty years ago. Enjoy making your party setting beautiful, with shimmering glasses and candles, lovely tableware and linens, fresh-cut flowers, and inspired food. But don't overdo it. Think of dressing a party like dressing yourself. Avoid too much jewelry. Keep it simple but stylish. (My mantra: In doubt? Leave it out.)

Be pretty—from the inside out. Always be kind. Never make people feel like impositions, even inadvertently. If anything, make your guests feel like inspirations. Ask more questions of them than they ask of you, and be genuinely interested in each person. It makes a difference.

CHAPTER TWO

PICK-ME-UPS:

Handheld Snacks

....

Allow me to introduce you to the finest in easy-to-eat appetizers for "free-range" party guests—folks untethered to utensils. The goal is to avoid this all-too-common scenario: Balancing a plate of goodies and a drink resembling a cruise ship pool in rough seas while conducting a polite but slightly skittish conversation and not catapulting your party fare.

Here you'll find the tried-and-true classics (cheese straws, deviled eggs, seasoned pecans) plus some newfangled goods (tartlet-style muffalettas, bite-size shrimp and grits with tomato jam). I can attest that all of it's worth a toast—one during which, delightfully, you'll have a free hand to join in!

Fanciful Cheese Straws

SERVES 8 TO 10, ABOUT FOUR STRAWS EACH

*Cheese straws, like spiced pecans, are Southern party classics (and also make nice food gifts).
Here, I've fashioned them into voluptuous ribbons, but you also can cut them into long, thin
"straws" or else chill the dough and slice it into wafers (a.k.a. "pennies") or into diamond or
heart shapes. Whatever form they take, you'll be happy that their flavor intensifies within a
day of preparing. Try them with Gruyère or Emmentaler cheese (instead of Cheddar) and a
pinch or two of nutmeg; it's truly yummy.*

½ cup butter, at room temperature
(see Cooking Notes)

2 cups shredded extra-sharp
Cheddar cheese (see
Cooking Notes, page 52)

1½ cups all-purpose flour

1 teaspoon salt

¼ teaspoon cayenne pepper, plus
more for dusting (optional)

¼ teaspoon smoked paprika, plus
more for dusting (optional)

¼ teaspoon ground black pepper

⅛ teaspoon garlic powder

Preheat the oven to 375°F. Line two baking sheets with parchment
paper and set aside.

Using a stand mixer fitted with the paddle attachment, beat the
butter and 1 cup of the cheese until it reaches a smooth, creamy
consistency, 5 to 7 minutes.

In a large bowl, sift together the flour, salt, cayenne, paprika, black
pepper, and garlic powder. Gradually add the flour mixture into the
cheese mixture, mixing well to blend them thoroughly.

When the dough is smooth, stir in the remaining 1 cup cheese.

Spoon the dough (which will have a putty-like texture) into a large
piping bag or cookie press fitted with a large star tip. Slowly pipe
3-inch-long strands of dough, shaping them curvaceously if desired,
onto the prepared baking sheets, spaced about 1½ inches apart.

Bake for 10 to 12 minutes, or until the edges begin to turn golden
brown. Remove the cheese straws from the oven and, if desired,
dust them with additional cayenne (for added heat) or paprika (for
color and subtle depth). Place the cheese straws on wire racks and
let them cool for 7 to 10 minutes.

Store in an airtight container, with parchment paper in between
the layers to protect from breakage, for up to 3 days at room temperature or up to 5 days in the refrigerator.

Cooking
Notes

*Butter softens faster when cut into slices and
placed on a warmed plate.*

*Thinner portions of cheese straw dough bake in
less time, so watch the oven.*

Just-Right Cocktail Pecans

SERVES 12, ABOUT ½ CUP EACH

Why people insist on turning pecans into wickedly womped-up, indestructible globs of complex seasonings is beyond me. These aren't too sweet or too spicy; they're just right for any gathering. They even get better over time.

1½ pounds pecan halves

½ cup unsalted butter

2 tablespoons brown or granulated sugar, plus more if needed

1 teaspoon ground cinnamon

1 teaspoon ground nutmeg

½ teaspoon ground black pepper

½ teaspoon cayenne pepper

Salt

Preheat the oven to 300°F.

Place the pecan halves in a medium bowl.

In a small sauté pan over low heat, melt the butter and stir in the brown sugar, cinnamon, nutmeg, black pepper, ¼ teaspoon of the cayenne, and 1 teaspoon salt. Once the sugar is dissolved, 1 to 2 minutes, remove the mixture from the heat.

Pour the mixture over the pecans and use a rubber spatula to gently combine and evenly coat the pecans.

Spread the seasoned pecans evenly on a large rimmed baking sheet and bake for 20 to 22 minutes, stirring every 5 minutes, shaking to even out the pecans on the pan before returning them to the oven. When the pecans are done they will be a dark golden brown and very aromatic. After removing the pecans from the oven, sprinkle the remaining ¼ teaspoon cayenne atop them and add more salt and sugar, if desired. Cool the seasoned pecans on a paper towel–lined pan.

Store in an airtight container for up to 1 week at room temperature or up to 1 month in the freezer.

Nut Job

• • •

Don't pay top dollar for seasoned nuts when you can make them at home. Place some shelled, raw nuts in a heavy-duty/cast-iron skillet and add a couple tablespoons of butter or safflower or olive oil. Sprinkle the nuts with, say, curry, cumin, and lime (especially nice on cashews) or rosemary-infused salt (on almonds in particular) and stir constantly until they're lightly coated and aromatic. Spoon them onto a rimmed baking sheet lined with foil or parchment and let cool. Store in an airtight container for up to 2 weeks.

Cajun-Seasoned Boiled Peanuts

SERVES 12 TO 14, ABOUT 1 CUP EACH

Funny how something as simple as boiled peanuts can get people so riled up over the best way to cook them. Some insist the only way to season them is at the cooling/soaking stage. Others believe the nuts should soak for up to three days beforehand. In any event, what we can all agree on is the joy in our hearts each autumn when handmade "Boiled P-Nuts" signs start cropping up on rural roadsides. Raw peanuts are sometimes called "green" despite the fact that they're not green. Look for them in supermarket produce sections or at farmers' markets. Serve either warm or at room temperature.

2 pounds in-shell raw "green" peanuts

½ cup Cajun seasoning

½ cup salt

6 tablespoons liquid Cajun-flavor shrimp and crab boil (I like Zatarain's; see Sources, page 138)

In a large (at least 12-quart) stockpot, combine the peanuts, Cajun seasoning, and enough water to cover the nuts. (To keep the peanuts submerged, place a Dutch oven lid or heavy plate atop them.) Soak them for 8 to 24 hours, then drain and rinse.

Add 4 to 5 quarts fresh water to the stockpot, along with the soaked peanuts, salt, and shrimp and crab boil. Bring them to a boil over high heat. Cover, turn the heat to medium-low, and cook until the peanuts are tender, 5 to 6 hours, stirring occasionally and adding more water to cover the peanuts when necessary.

Remove the seasoned peanuts from the heat, let them stand in the stockpot for at least 1 hour, and then drain.

Store in an airtight container for up to 1 week in the refrigerator or several months in the freezer.

Old Salts

• • •

Cajun seasoning, also known as Creole seasoning, tends to be salty, which is why I like the well-seasoned but lower-in-sodium "Essence" or "Bayou Blast" blends sold by Chef Emeril Lagasse and the "Lite" version of Tony Chachere's (pronounced "SASH-uh-ree's"). Emeril's seasonings are richer in paprika, while the ones by Tony have a tad more red pepper. You'll never regret having to add a bit more salt to a dish—unlike realizing you've overdone it and can't take that salt away. See Sources, page 138.

Fried Black-Eyed Peas

SERVES 6 TO 8, ABOUT ½ CUP EACH

The first time I savored airy, fried to crisp-tender black-eyed peas, I was at the now-defunct Roswell, Georgia, eatery Relish. Restaurateur Andy Badgett's recipe, involving dried black-eyed peas and a number of soaking/seasoning steps, was fabulous. But truthfully, it was time-consuming. After hearing about a friend's success with frozen and thawed black-eyed peas, I was encouraged. Then another friend raved about using canned and rinsed ones. Boy, was I ever pleased to discover that both options are not only super-simple, but absolutely delicious. Leftover peas will stay crisp for about 1 day in a bowl at room temperature, loosely covered with plastic wrap.

Canola or vegetable oil for frying

4 cups frozen and thawed black-eyed peas or two 15.5-ounce cans, rinsed, drained, and thoroughly dried

4 teaspoons seafood seasoning (I like Old Bay)

Salt

In a large heavy skillet, Dutch oven, or electric fryer, add canola oil to a depth of at least 3 inches and heat it to 360°F. Line a baking sheet with paper towels.

Carefully lower 2 cups of the peas into the oil and cook until they are thoroughly hot and crispy, about 4 minutes. (The peas will begin to float and hiss when ready.) Remove them with a slotted spoon to the prepared baking sheet. Repeat with the remaining 2 cups peas.

Place the fried peas in a medium bowl and toss them with the seafood seasoning. Season with salt and toss. The peas are best served hot or warm.

Lucky Charm

• • •

Black-eyed peas are eaten on New Year's Day to bring good luck in the coming year. The superstition derives from several stories, the most popular of which involves the legume—actually more akin to lentils than peas—surviving Union soldiers' rampage of Southern crops during the Civil War (thus representing survival). In West Africa, where black-eyed peas (better known as "cowpeas") have long been seen as bringing good luck, babies are sometimes fed a spoonful of the mashed, nutrient-rich food. Another story has it that the peas' representation of success-via-humility stems from the Sephardic Jews who first settled Georgia in the 1730s; they ate the peas during the Jewish New Year (Rosh Hashanah).

Debonaire Deviled Eggs

SERVES 8 TO 12, TWO OR THREE HALVES EACH

I grew up thinking of these as "bedeviled" eggs after witnessing one too many boiled-egg massacres by my mother. She called them "hard-bald" eggs—which to my young mind made perfect sense; but what didn't make sense was how she got them to be so pitted, dented, cracked, and torn, unlike my friends' mothers' eggs. Thus, I spent many years being intimidated by the process until I learned the secret to making them look, and taste, darn near perfect. (One of the tricks involves a pushpin.)

---

12 large eggs (see Cooking Note)

¼ cup mayonnaise

4 slices bacon, cooked and crumbled (optional)

3 tablespoons sweet pickle relish

2 teaspoons prepared mustard

¼ teaspoon salt

⅛ teaspoon ground black pepper

Sprigs of fresh savory or another herb for garnish (optional)

Turn the eggs bottom- (wider-) side up in the carton. Use a pushpin to delicately poke one hole squarely in each center.

Fill a large saucepan or small Dutch oven with 2 to 2½ quarts of water (enough to cover the eggs; use two pans if cooking all the eggs at once). Bring the water to a rolling boil.

Use a slotted spoon to add six eggs to the pan (working quickly but carefully to get them in at the same time); boil the eggs for 6 minutes.

Remove the pan from the heat. Let the eggs sit for 6 minutes (for slightly soft yolks; add about 40 seconds for firmer yolks).

Remove each egg with a slotted spoon and place it on a kitchen towel. Repeat with the remaining six eggs. Let the eggs cool to room temperature, about 20 minutes, before peeling. (Store in the refrigerator, unpeeled, for up to 1 week; peeled, for up to 4 days.)

Peel the eggs under cool running water. Slice the eggs in half lengthwise, gently scooping out the yolks into a medium bowl. Add the mayonnaise, three-fourths of the crumbled bacon (if using), pickle relish, mustard, salt, and pepper. Stir to combine (and adjust the seasonings as desired). Use a small spoon (or better yet, a piping bag) to insert the filling into the egg halves. Garnish with the remaining chopped bacon and savory, if desired, before serving.

Cooking Note

Large eggs are best used for egg plates and are easier to eat in one or two bites.

Muffaletta Bites

SERVES 6 TO 8, THREE OR FOUR TARTLETS EACH

God help us if we ever have to do without olive salad, a tangy veggie confetti that perks up everything it graces. Though it's hard to beat the crunchy Italian-sandwich behemoths (pronounced "muffa-lottas" by New Orleans locals) at Central Grocery in the French Quarter, it's easy to want to eat any semblance thereof. These flavorful little puffs do the trick.

One 16-ounce jar Italian olive salad, drained

½ cup shredded smoked Provolone cheese

¼ cup finely chopped salami

¼ cup finely chopped ham

Two 12-ounce cans refrigerated flaky biscuit dough

Fresh Italian flat-leaf parsley for garnish

In a medium bowl, stir together the olive salad with the cheese, salami, and ham. Cover and refrigerate for about 1 hour.

Preheat the oven to 350°F. Lightly coat two 12-well miniature muffin pans with cooking spray, if necessary.

On a lightly floured surface, place the biscuit dough in two even rows and use a rolling pin or clean fingers to gently flatten/pat into a ½-inch-thick rectangle. Firmly press the perforations to seal. Cut each rectangle into 24 squares (each about 2 inches wide).

Place one square of dough in each of the prepared muffin wells. Firmly press the dough into the bottom and up the sides, leaving the corners of the dough extended over the edges of each well; shape the edges with your fingers or use a fork to crimp it as desired. (The dough will rise at times; just press it back down until you can add filling. At this point, you can cover the muffin pan and refrigerate for up to 1 hour.)

Spoon a heaping 1 tablespoon of the filling into each well.

Bake until golden brown, 10 to 12 minutes. Let cool for 5 minutes. Remove the tartlets from the pan and garnish each with a parsley leaf. Serve warm or at room temperature.

Olive Groove
• • •

I like to use Boscoli Family Italian Olive Salad for this recipe. It's a medley of pickled cauliflower, carrots, celery, green olives, black olives, and capers, combined with a special blend of spices and select oils and handmade using a 100-year-old family recipe. See Sources, page 138.

Shrimp & Gritlets with Emeril's Tomato Jam

SERVES 12, ABOUT THREE GRITLETS EACH

These cheese grit tartlets are topped with scrumptious savory-sweet tomato jam and tender bite-size shrimp. The bacon is optional, but it adds so much flavor. C'est si bon.

2 cups chicken broth

1 cup half-and-half or milk

1 cup uncooked regular or quick-cooking grits (but not instant)

2 tablespoons butter

¼ to ½ cup finely chopped green bell pepper

¼ cup finely diced red onion

2 garlic cloves, minced

2½ teaspoons Cajun seasoning

½ cup shredded white Cheddar or Parmesan cheese

½ cup cooked, crumbled bacon (optional)

36 medium (41/50 count) shrimp, peeled and deveined

¾ cup Emeril's Tomato Jam (recipe follows)

Finely sliced green onions cut on the bias for garnish (optional)

Preheat the oven to 350°F. Lightly grease three 12-well miniature muffin pans.

In a saucepan over medium-high heat, bring the broth and half-and-half to a boil. Gradually whisk in the grits and return the mixture to a boil, stirring once. Turn the heat to low, cover the pan, and let the grits simmer, stirring occasionally, until thickened, 5 to 10 minutes. Remove the pan from the heat; cover and set aside.

In a skillet over medium-high heat, melt 1 tablespoon of the butter. Add the bell pepper, red onion, garlic, and ½ teaspoon of the Cajun seasoning; sauté the vegetables until tender, 4 to 6 minutes.

Stir the vegetables into the grits along with the cheese and bacon (if using).

Spoon a heaping 1 tablespoonful of the grits mixture into each well of the muffin pans, pressing the mixture into the bottom and lightly up the sides.

Bake the gritlets until lightly browned, 20 to 25 minutes. Remove the pans from the oven.

Using the back of a small spoon, create an indentation in the center of each gritlet and remove them from the pans. Let cool completely on wire racks, 20 to 30 minutes. (At this point, you can refrigerate them for up to a day in an airtight container with each layer separated by sheets of wax paper. Slowly reheat them in a 225°F oven.)

In a large skillet over medium-high heat, melt the remaining 1 tablespoon butter. Add the shrimp and sprinkle them with the remaining 2 teaspoons Cajun seasoning. Cook the shrimp just until they turn pink, 3 to 5 minutes.

Arrange the gritlets on a platter. Top each one with a heaping 1 teaspoon of the tomato jam and one shrimp. Garnish with sliced green onions, if desired. Serve immediately.

Gritty Details

• • •

Grits labeled "regular" have a medium texture and take about 10 minutes to cook. "Quick-cooking" grits are ground slightly finer and cook in about 5 minutes. "Instant" grits, which are pre-cooked and dehydrated (plumping up instantly with boiling water), have a disagreeably artificial flavor and a thin texture that won't make for a sturdy tart. On the opposite end of the spectrum are coarse white or yellow "stone-ground" grits, which can take up to an hour to cook.

Emeril's Tomato Jam

MAKES ABOUT 1 CUP

This recipe, adapted from one by Chef Emeril Lagasse, is an updated alternative to hot-pepper jelly.

2 cups diced tomatoes

1 cup rice wine vinegar

¼ cup light corn syrup

2 tablespoons sugar

2 tablespoons honey

1 tablespoon minced garlic

⅛ to ¼ teaspoon cayenne pepper

In a medium saucepan, stir to combine the tomatoes, vinegar, corn syrup, sugar, honey, garlic, and cayenne and bring the mixture to a boil. Lower the heat to a simmer and cook, stirring occasionally, until most of the liquid has evaporated, 30 to 35 minutes.

Remove the pan from the heat and let the tomato jam cool to room temperature. Store in an airtight container in the refrigerator for up to 2 weeks.

Rhapsody in Blue, Fig & Rustic Ham

SERVES 12, TWO OR THREE TOASTS EACH

Blue cheese, sweet figs, and cured ham are a stellar combination. If your cheese is very cold, make it easier to spread by softening it in the microwave for 5 or 6 seconds (let it go past 10 and you'll have a nuclear meltdown). If the cheese's flavor is too overpowering for you (sans the goodies on top), add a bit of butter to make it milder (but more gooey). Some like this drizzled with a light honey, but I think it's superb just like this.

24 to 36 Toasted Crostini (page 81; see Cooking Notes, this page)

10 ounces crumbled creamy blue cheese (I like Gorgonzola)

One 8.5-ounce container fig spread or thick preserves (see Cooking Notes)

1 teaspoon chopped fresh thyme, plus thyme sprigs for garnish (optional)

8 to 10 very thin slices country ham or prosciutto

Preheat the oven to 400°F. Line a baking sheet with parchment paper or a silicone baking mat.

Spread the crostini on the prepared baking sheet. Spread 1 to 2 teaspoons of the cheese atop each crostini, then add a heaping 1 teaspoon of the fig spread, a pinch of chopped thyme, and a folded section of country ham. Bake until the cheese is bubbly and melted, 5 to 7 minutes. Garnish with thyme sprigs, if desired. Serve hot, warm, or at room temperature.

Cooking Notes

When making the toasts, bake the crostini a few minutes less than you normally would, since they'll be returning to the oven with toppings.

Dalmatia's fig spread is rich in Croatian figs— and now that they're adding orange, it's over-the-moon delicious. (See Sources, page 138.) To substitute with fig preserves, drain some of the preserves' liquid if necessary.

Wee Chicken & Waffles with Jezebel-Maple Syrup

SERVES 10 TO 12, THREE OR FOUR WAFFLES EACH

Sure, you can make your own bite-size waffles in a special waffle iron, and you can fry your own chicken tenders, but since good commercially available versions are easy to find, do yourself a favor: Pick up others' handiwork to pair with this vivacious, easy-to-make syrup. The tiny treats always get a fun reception, especially as tailgate snacks. Prepared horseradish, a pungent mush of grated horseradish, vinegar, and salt, is most often found in small jars somewhere near a supermarket's cheese case. It's not to be confused with the "creamy horseradish" spread in the mustard aisle.

JEZEBEL-MAPLE SYRUP

2 cups maple syrup

¼ cup pineapple preserves

¼ cup apple jelly

1½ tablespoons prepared horseradish

¾ teaspoon ground black pepper

½ teaspoon salt

40 mini waffles from a 10.9-ounce package, lightly toasted

40 pieces cooked fried popcorn chicken

Finely chopped fresh Italian flat-leaf parsley or green onion for garnish (optional)

Hot sauce for serving

To make the syrup: In a large microwave-safe glass measuring cup with pour spout (one holding at least 3 cups) or a bowl, add the maple syrup, pineapple preserves, apple jelly, horseradish, pepper, and salt; whisk to combine.

Microwave the mixture on high for 35 seconds. (You can also heat it in a small saucepan on low until the mixture is warm.) Stir and taste, adjusting the flavor if desired. Set the syrup aside.

Place the toasted waffles on a large serving platter. Top each waffle with a piece of chicken. Drizzle the chicken-waffle bites with about 1 teaspoon of the syrup. Garnish with the parsley, if desired, and serve with the remaining syrup and hot sauce.

Sticking Point

• • •

Despite its Southern culinary roots, the chicken 'n' waffles craze took a while to actually catch on *in* the South. Long known as special occasion "soul food" for African Americans outside the region, the unique food pairing was first popularized in 1930s New York City, at places like the Wells Supper Club and Tillie's Chicken Shack in Harlem. Within forty years, Los Angeles would flip for it after Roscoe's House of Chicken 'N Waffles was opened by former Harlem resident Herb Hudson in 1975 in the Long Beach area. It now boasts a cult following across the nation.

Buttermilk-Battered Okra Fries with Comeback Sauce

SERVES 6, ABOUT SIX FRIES EACH; MAKES 2 CUPS SAUCE

If people think they don't like okra, it's usually because they haven't had it in season (May through September) or otherwise fried right. I know—I used to be one of the people who could only stomach it encased (read: hidden) in a fortress of cornmeal. And while I still like it that way, I'm fonder of slicing okra lengthwise like "fries," and using a light buttermilk-and-flour-based batter to help show off okra's curves and seedy charm. I've paired it here with Comeback Sauce, but it's also good with Creole Rémoulade Sauce (page 39) or Goodly Ranch Dip (page 58).

COMEBACK SAUCE

1 cup mayonnaise

¼ cup chili sauce

¼ cup ketchup

¼ cup extra-virgin olive oil

2 garlic cloves, minced,
or ¼ teaspoon garlic powder

2 tablespoons finely grated
sweet or white onion or
¼ teaspoon onion powder

1 tablespoon Worcestershire sauce

1 tablespoon freshly squeezed
lemon juice

1 teaspoon Dijon or yellow mustard

1 teaspoon ground black pepper

1 teaspoon hot sauce

¼ teaspoon hot or smoked paprika

Salt (optional)

To make the sauce: In a food processor, purée the mayonnaise, chili sauce, ketchup, olive oil, garlic, onion, Worcestershire, lemon juice, mustard, black pepper, hot sauce, and paprika. (Or use a medium bowl and whisk to combine all the ingredients.) Season with salt, if needed, cover tightly, and let the sauce sit overnight in the refrigerator before serving.

To make the okra: Place several layers of paper towels atop a paper bag or platter. Keep it close to where you'll be frying.

In an electric fryer, Dutch oven, or heavy cast-iron skillet, add canola oil to a depth of 2 to 4 inches. Heat to 350°F. (If not using an electric fryer, use a fry/candy thermometer to ensure the temperature stays consistent.)

In a medium bowl, soak the sliced okra in the buttermilk and set aside.

In a paper bag or large plastic zip-top bag, combine the flour, cornstarch, ½ teaspoon salt, black pepper, garlic powder, and cayenne (if using).

Drain the buttermilk-soaked okra and dredge it in the flour mixture. Carefully shake off any excess flour.

Continued

OKRA FRIES

Canola or corn oil for frying

8 ounces small to medium okra pods, stemmed and halved lengthwise

1 cup buttermilk (or enough to cover okra)

1 cup all-purpose flour

¾ cup cornstarch

Salt

½ teaspoon ground black pepper

½ teaspoon garlic powder

¼ teaspoon cayenne pepper (optional)

Fry the okra in batches of seven or eight pieces for 2 to 3 minutes, or until crispy and light golden brown, turning them carefully midway through.

Use a fry basket or slotted spoon to remove the okra to drain on the paper towels. While still hot, season the okra with additional salt, if desired.

Serve the okra fries immediately with the sauce.

Good Comeback
• • •

The Mississippi classic Comeback Sauce, a peppier cousin of rémoulade and Thousand Island dressing, is thought to have originated in the late 1920s or early '30s at Jackson's first Greek restaurant, The Rotisserie. And named for the notion that it makes you want to "come back" for more.

Fried Catfish Po' Babies with Creole Rémoulade Sauce

SERVES 12; MAKES ABOUT 2 CUPS SAUCE

Diminutive po' boys, or "po' babies," can nicely show off fried catfish fillet curls—the "up-do" flips created during frying. A fine yet rugged crust on this fish keeps the fillets in good shape, as does the paper wrapping, exposing just enough of the sandwich's innate beauty and flavor while also making it easily portable for tailgating events and picnics. Low-protein cake flour or Wondra yields a crispier crust—always a plus for fried catfish. Just make sure to marinate the fish for 8 hours before cooking. For sandwich wrapping, you'll need twelve pieces of butcher or freezer paper, cut into 6$\frac{1}{2}$-by-15-inch strips, and twelve pieces of ribbon or twine.

. . .

Twelve 4- to 5-ounce or six 9-ounce thin-cut farm-raised catfish fillets, halved

1½ cups buttermilk

½ to 1 teaspoon hot sauce (optional, but good)

CREOLE RÉMOULADE SAUCE

1 to 1¼ cups mayonnaise

¼ to ⅓ cup Creole mustard

2 tablespoons prepared horse-radish (see headnote, page 35)

2 to 3 tablespoons chopped fresh Italian flat-leaf parsley

2 tablespoons freshly squeezed lemon juice

1 tablespoon sweet paprika

1 or 2 small shallots, minced

1 teaspoon mild hot sauce

¼ to ½ teaspoon salt

¼ to ½ teaspoon ground black pepper

¼ teaspoon cayenne pepper (optional)

Rinse the catfish fillets and dry using paper towels. In a small bowl, whisk together the buttermilk and hot sauce (if using). Place the catfish in a single layer in a 9-by-13-inch baking dish; pour the buttermilk mixture over the fish. Cover and refrigerate for 8 hours, turning once. (A buttermilk marinade enhances the flavor of the fish.)

To make the sauce: In a medium bowl, combine the mayonnaise, Creole mustard, horseradish, parsley, lemon juice, paprika, shallots, hot sauce, salt, black pepper, and cayenne (if using) and stir to mix. Adjust the seasonings as desired. (Store in an airtight container in the refrigerator for up to 1 day.)

In a medium bowl, combine half of the rémoulade and the coleslaw mix; stir to combine. Cover and chill the slaw and remaining sauce at least 1 hour, or overnight, to let the flavors meld.

Let the fish fillets stand at room temperature for 10 minutes.

In an electric fryer, large Dutch oven, or deep cast-iron skillet, add peanut oil to a depth of 2 to 3 inches. Heat to 360°F. (If not using an electric fryer, use a fry/candy termometer to ensure the temperature stays consistent.)

In a pie plate or shallow dish, stir to combine the cornmeal, flour, salt, black pepper, Cajun seasoning, cayenne, garlic powder, and paprika (if using).

Continued

One 16-ounce bag coleslaw mix
(red and green cabbage
with carrots)

Peanut oil for frying

½ to ¾ cup plain yellow cornmeal

½ cup cake flour or Wondra flour

1½ teaspoons salt

1 teaspoon ground black pepper

1 teaspoon Cajun seasoning

½ to 1 teaspoon cayenne pepper

¼ to ½ teaspoon garlic powder

1 teaspoon paprika (optional)

12 bolillo rolls (see Cooking Note)

Remove the fish from the buttermilk mixture, allowing excess liquid to drip off. Dredge the fillets in the cornmeal mixture, shaking off the excess.

Fry the fillets, in batches of two whole ones or four small portions, until golden brown, turning once, 5 to 6 minutes. (To create fillet curls, place each fillet in the oil so that part of one edge rests upward along the side of a fry basket or skillet; you also can use tongs to hold the curl in place until it's set.) Remove the fish from the oil with a large slotted spoon.

Transfer the cooked fillets to a wire rack fitted into a rimmed pan. Keep warm, uncovered, in a 225°F oven until ready to serve.

Cut the rolls in half and, if necessary, lightly toast them (brushing the interiors with olive oil or melted butter, if desired).

Add ⅓ cup of the slaw to each roll and top with a catfish portion, curl-side extended. Spoon 1 tablespoon of the remaining rémoulade on the catfish and top with the upper half of the roll.

Place each sandwich at the end of a paper strip, leaving about 1 inch or so exposed (preferably showing the catfish curl); fold up to encase and use invisible tape to seal. Tie ribbon around each wrapped sandwich and serve ASAP.

Cooking
Note

Oval bolillo rolls are similar to French baguettes, with crunchy buttery exteriors and soft interiors. They're available in Mexican or large supermarkets. Substitute with other 5- to 6-inch French-style rolls.

Corndog Pups with Honey of a Mustard Sauce

SERVES 10, ABOUT FOUR PUPS EACH; MAKES 1½ CUPS SAUCE

These little charmers are winning tailgating treats. They sport a fun look, can be made in advance, and hold up pretty well (quite literally). Making them is easy but time-consuming without some kitchen assistance via family or friends to help you get a handle on them (again, quite literally). For the dipping sauce, yellow mustard's fine, but honey mustard is finer—and offers a sweeter tanginess. For the skewers, cut eleven 12-inch bamboo wood skewers into fourths.

HONEY OF A MUSTARD SAUCE

¾ cup Dijon mustard

½ cup mayonnaise, plus more if needed

¼ cup honey, plus more if needed

⅛ teaspoon cayenne pepper (optional)

CORNDOG PUPS

One 14-ounce package cocktail-size smoked beef sausages

Vegetable oil for frying

3 tablespoons bacon drippings (see Cooking Notes)

½ cup all-purpose flour

⅓ cup yellow cornmeal

¾ teaspoon baking powder

½ teaspoon salt

¼ teaspoon baking soda

1 egg

1¼ cups buttermilk

To make the sauce: In a medium bowl, whisk together the mustard, mayonnaise, honey, and cayenne (if using). Taste and adjust the flavor and consistency with more mayonnaise and honey, as desired. Cover and chill at least 1 hour before serving. (Store in an airtight container in the refrigerator for up to 1 week.)

To make the corndog pups: Line two plates with paper towels.

Insert a skewer into each sausage, leaving 1 inch of each skewer exposed. Place the skewered sausages on one of the prepared plates to drain. Set aside.

In an electric fryer; Dutch oven; or large, deep, heavy skillet, add vegetable oil to a depth of 3 to 4 inches. Add 2 tablespoons of the bacon drippings and heat to 375°F. (If not using an electric fryer, use a fry/candy thermometer to ensure the temperature stays consistent.)

In a medium bowl, whisk together the flour, cornmeal, baking powder, salt, and baking soda.

In another medium bowl (preferably one with a pour spout, like a 2-cup glass measuring cup), lightly beat the egg. Add the buttermilk and remaining 1 tablespoon bacon drippings (make sure the drippings aren't piping hot or your milk will curdle). Stir in the dry ingredients. (The mixture will begin to get somewhat foamy and rise.) Pour some of the mixture into a smaller measuring cup or coffee mug, which will nicely hold the sausages in the batter without the skewers becoming submerged.

Dip four or five skewered sausages into the batter, making sure each sausage is covered thoroughly. (The batter should be thick enough to coat the sausages without much sliding off.) Take one sausage by the skewer, twirling it a bit to evenly coat and allow any excess coating to drip back into the cup.

Holding the end of the stick, carefully place the sausage straight down into the oil to quickly seal it before releasing it to float around in the oil. Quickly repeat with the other skewered sausages. Cook until the corndogs are evenly golden brown, using a slotted spoon to gently turn them in the oil, 2 to 3 minutes.

Remove each corndog from the oil and place it on the second prepared plate to drain.

Serve the corndog pups with the sauce.

Cooking Notes

Don't exclude the bacon drippings, which give the pups that made-at-the-carnival flavor.

The corndogs look and taste their best if eaten within 2 hours of cooking. (If necessary, refrigerate the cooked corndogs between layers of wax paper in an airtight container up to 24 hours before serving. To reheat, cook them in a 200°F oven on a baking sheet fitted with a wire rack for 15 to 17 minutes, turning halfway through to ensure even heating.)

Lil' Natchitoches Meat Pies

SERVES 8 TO 10, TWO OR THREE PIES EACH

First, the pronunciation: "KNACK-a-tish." If the historic north-central Louisiana town looks like a microcosm of New Orleans' French Quarter, it's because, actually, the Vieux Carré looks similar to it! Natchitoches was built four years before New Orleans, making it the oldest permanent settlement in the Louisiana Purchase. With beef, pork, garlic, and other seasonings, these meat pies are akin to empanadas filled with spicy picadillo meat like those prepared in Louisiana during the Spanish rule in the late eighteenth century. Pair them with Goodly Ranch Dip (page 58), which can be amped up with more parsley or substituted with cilantro to both stand up to and soothe the meat's bold flavor.

FILLING

1 teaspoon vegetable oil

12 ounces lean ground beef (see Cooking Notes)

12 ounces ground pork (see Cooking Notes)

½ cup chopped onion

½ cup chopped celery

½ cup chopped red bell pepper

1 teaspoon lower-sodium Cajun seasoning

1 teaspoon salt

½ teaspoon ground black pepper

¼ teaspoon cayenne pepper

4 to 6 garlic cloves, minced

1 tablespoon all-purpose flour

1 cup beef broth or water

½ cup chopped green onions

To make the filling: In a large skillet over medium heat, warm the vegetable oil and cook the beef and pork, stirring occasionally, until browned, 5 to 6 minutes. Add the onion, celery, bell pepper, Cajun seasoning, salt, black pepper, and cayenne and cook, stirring often, until the vegetables are tender, about 10 minutes. Add the garlic and cook for an additional 3 minutes.

In a small bowl, stir the flour into the beef broth until it dissolves. Add the flour slurry to the meat mixture and simmer until slightly thickened. Add the green onions and stir to combine; adjust the seasonings as desired. Remove the mixture from the heat and let cool completely. (Note: If the mixture looks greasy, drain it in a colander. At this point, you can store it in an airtight container in the refrigerator for up to 3 days.)

To make the pastry: In a medium to large bowl, sift together the flour, salt, and baking powder. Cut in the shortening until the mixture resembles coarse meal. In a small bowl, beat 1 egg with the ³⁄₄ cup milk. Gradually stir the egg mixture into the flour mixture, working it to make a thick but pliable dough. (At this point, you can store the dough tightly wrapped in plastic wrap in the refrigerator for up to 1 day. Let it reach room temperature before using.)

Divide the dough into twenty-four equal portions. On a floured surface using a floured rolling pin, roll each portion of dough into a thin round about 3½ inches in diameter.

D'OH BOY PASTRY

3 cups all-purpose flour

1½ teaspoons salt

¾ teaspoon baking powder

6 tablespoons vegetable shortening

2 eggs

¾ cup milk, plus 1 tablespoon

Vegetable oil for frying

In a small bowl, lightly beat the remaining egg with the remaining 1 tablespoon milk to make an egg wash; set aside.

Place 1 tablespoon of filling in the center of each dough round. (Don't overfill or you'll have a mess.) Fold the edges together, pressing out any air, and crimp to seal with a fork. (At this point, you can store the pies, separated in sandwich bags, in an airtight container in the refrigerator for up to 2 days, or in the freezer for up to 2 months. Do not thaw before frying or baking.)

In an electric fryer; Dutch oven; or deep, heavy skillet, add vegetable oil to a depth of several inches. Heat to 360°F. (If not using an electric fryer, use a fry/candy thermometer to ensure the temperature stays consistent.)

Brush the pies lightly with the egg wash. Fry the pies in batches until golden brown, turning with a slotted spoon to ensure even cooking, 3 to 4 minutes. Drain them on paper towels and let cool about 5 minutes before serving. These don't store well, so eat them while they are hot!

Cooking Notes

Unless you use at least 90/10 lean-to-fat ratio meat, the filling will be too greasy.

Ground pork is not ground pork sausage, which is already (strongly) seasoned.

When you're short on time, Goya's pre-made empanada turnover puff pastry disks (thawed from frozen) make fine substitutes.

STUFF OF LEGEND: FINGER SANDWICHES

Finger sandwiches—the two-bite delectables more commonly called "tea" or "party" sandwiches—became fashionable in 1840s England to help stave off hunger while enjoying mid-afternoon tea. The idea caught on in this country but, over time, the fare has increasingly gotten larger. Friends, know this: It's just fine to follow the long-held rule that the layer of filling shouldn't exceed the thickness of the bread. You won't look like you're skimping. And we'll look relieved not to have to fumble with portly, overstuffed snacks. And as for the tea? Iced and sweet will work just fine.

Inside Scoop

Consider these fillings and freely mix and match with the following bread choices.

- Delicate, fine-textured vegetables—very thinly sliced cucumbers, radishes, and exquisitely sculptural feather-light watercress

- Jam and butter

- Sweet, tender ham (preferably with a light coating of Mustard Butter, see page 102)

- Cheese spreads (think cream cheese and golden raisins with honey or mango chutney, or homemade herbed cream cheeses or commercially available ones like Boursin)

- Richly flavored chicken salads with the likes of sliced grapes, herbs, lemon zest, and chopped pecans (see Curried Chicken Salad, page 49)

- Sliced, tender turkey with apricot chutney

- Best Pimiento Cheese (page 52)

- Bacon, lettuce, tomato, and extra-good mayo

- Finely chopped egg salad with chives or sliced green olives

- Cucumber, goat cheese, and mint

- Turkey, cream cheese, and slivered basil (especially nice on raisin bread)

- Ham, brie, and thinly sliced green apple

- Watercress and radish with a hint of salt (lovely during winter)

- Prosciutto with blue cheese and butter spread (50/50 ratio) and thinly sliced pears

- Roast beef, Mustard Butter (see page 102), and a spinach leaf or two

- Camembert or brie and fig preserves

- Shrimp puréed with mayonnaise and flavored with curry

- Blue cheese or cream cheese with sliced grapes, walnuts, and dried cranberries

- Goat cheese blended with roasted vegetable purée

- Cream cheese blended with strawberries, raspberries, and pineapple

- Brie or cream cheese with raspberry or apricot jam on raisin bread

Continued

The Best Breads

These breads work best for small finger sandwiches. Inspect darker breads for freshness to avoid them being stale and tough.

- Biscuits
- Cocktail bread (in the grocery deli section)
- Multigrain or seeded wheat
- Pretzel bread or buns
- Pumpernickel
- Raisin
- Swirled rye
- Tortillas in various colors
- White or wheat bread, slightly firm, thinly sliced (e.g., Pepperidge Farm) or soft (e.g., Wonder Bread)
- Yeast rolls

Prep Talk

- Avoid sandwich "sog" and dried-up bread: If at all possible, make the fillings in advance and cut bread portions shortly before serving. Most fillings can be made up to a day ahead and kept refrigerated in airtight containers. Breads and some pre-made sandwiches (those without much ooze factor) can be separated by layers of wax paper, covered with a damp tea towel or paper towels, and kept in an airtight container. Before serving at slightly cool or room temperature, add another damp towel covering to keep bread moist; remove just before serving. Use a pastry brush to spread lightly melted (but not hot) European-style butter (e.g., Plugrá) on each bread slice as a "sealant" before adding other toppings.

- Cool fillings spread more easily when softened to room temperature.

- Freezing bread until just-firm (but not icy) makes it easier to cut into sections.

- For neat edges, use a serrated knife to remove crusts after filling sandwiches.

- Count on three or four tea sandwiches per person if offering other fare.

- Cut bread into squares, rectangles, or triangles before filling. You also can use biscuit or cookie cutters to make rounds, and more unique shapes like diamonds and hearts (which are fun for card games). Serve different types of bread squares or triangles in a checkerboard, or other graphically and visually appealing fashion.

- Coat sandwich sides with a light layer of butter or mayo before rolling them in, say, minced fresh parsley or dill; finely chopped pecans or thin slices of almonds; sweet paprika; or soft plain bread crumbs or panko.

- For tortillas (spinach, red chile, etc.), evenly spread a thin layer of desired filling (flavored cream cheese with ham, for instance) onto one side; roll, cover tightly with plastic wrap, and chill for about an hour. Slice into rounds to serve.

Curried Chicken Salad

Whipped cream in the mayo and golden raisins plumped by orange juice make this a swoon-worthy sandwich filling on just about any bread. It's also lovely in little phyllo cups or endive leaves. One 2- to 3-pound rotisserie chicken will yield 3 to 4 cups diced chicken. Use regular curry powder for this; anything marked "Madras" will be too hot and overpower the delicate balance of this recipe.

¼ cup freshly squeezed orange juice

½ cup golden raisins

¼ cup whipping cream

1 cup mayonnaise

1 tablespoon curry powder

¼ to ½ teaspoon salt

¼ teaspoon ground black pepper

3 cups diced cooked chicken

½ cup sliced almonds, lightly toasted (see page 89), plus more for garnish

¼ cup finely chopped celery

¼ cup finely sliced green onions

In a small oven-safe bowl or glass measuring cup, heat the orange juice in the microwave on high for about 30 seconds. Add the raisins and press down to ensure the liquid reaches the top of the raisins so they're completely covered. Let the raisins soak for about 10 minutes before draining them.

In a large bowl with high sides, use a handheld mixer to whip the cream until soft peaks form. Use a spatula to fold in the mayonnaise. Stir in the curry powder, salt, and pepper. Add the chicken, almonds, celery, green onions, and plumped raisins. Gently combine and refrigerate at least 3 hours, or overnight, for flavors to meld.

CHAPTER THREE

SPREAD THE WORD:

Dips, Spreads, and Salsas

....

Gathered here are Southern dips and spreads with magnetism and flavor of the highest order. It'll just be up to you to doll them up with decorative platters and serving utensils, enlist a chafing dish or ice-bed to keep them warm and gooey or cold and fresh, and offer them with any number of "base hits" for helping them go the distance (to mouths). And as a plus for the host, most of these recipes not only can be made a day or so in advance, but actually taste better if you do just that.

Fortunately, gone are the days of setting out dips only to see them become the personal grazing post for those prone to elbow others and double-dip to their heart's content. Now there are myriad ideas for allowing people to dive in and dash off. Plates of crispy whatnots can be made portable with sauces in little cups or spreads spooned into ramekins or small glass canning jars.

To get you thinking about what to pair with your dips and spreads, here's a roundup of edible servers to put them on pedestals of sorts.

- Buttery or whole-grain crackers

- Canapé bread slices

- Cornbread sticks or mini muffins

- Endive leaves

- Lavash crackers or bread slices toasted with oil, herbs, and/or Parmesan cheese

- Melba toast or lightly toasted party bread

- Multicolored tortilla or root-vegetable chips

- Pita or bagel chips

- Raisin bread slices

- Sliced fruit (green or red apples or pears)

- Sliced vegetables (squash, zucchini, cucumber, and/or celery)

- Toasted wedges of pita or naan bread

- Water or pita crackers

Best Pimiento Cheese

MAKES ABOUT 2½ CUPS; ENOUGH FOR TWELVE SERVINGS OR ABOUT 24 FINGER SANDWICHES

Some people like their pimiento cheese mayonnaise-y, but I like just enough mayo to keep freshly grated, good-quality cheese clinging together for dear life. In this recipe, hints of fresh jalapeño, sweet onion, and garlic add zip, while cucumber slices and celery ribs make crisp, cool hosts for the spread. Use a vegetable peeler to remove strips of skin from the cucumber before slicing it into rounds to create a striking effect.

⅓ cup mayonnaise,
plus more if needed

One 4-ounce jar pimientos, drained

¼ cup finely chopped sweet onion

1 small jalapeño pepper,
seeded and minced

1 garlic clove, minced

⅛ to ¼ teaspoon hot sauce
(optional)

⅛ teaspoon ground white pepper
(optional)

1 cup shredded extra-sharp
white Cheddar cheese
(see Cooking Notes)

1 cup shredded medium
yellow Cheddar cheese
(see Cooking Notes)

Ground sea salt (optional;
see Cooking Notes)

Celery leaves for garnish (optional)

In a medium bowl, combine the mayonnaise, pimientos, onion, jalapeño, garlic, and hot sauce and white pepper (if using). Add both grated cheeses and gently stir the mixture until it reaches your desired consistency, adding more mayonnaise if necessary.

Cover and refrigerate the pimiento cheese for about 2 hours to let the flavors meld. Adjust the mayonnaise consistency, season with sea salt if necessary, and garnish with celery leaves, if desired, before serving.

Cooking Notes

Packaged grated cheese contains "powdered cellulose," or wood pulp, to keep it from sticking (which isn't the objective here). It therefore looks, and tastes, better to shred cheese from a block of it just before preparing.

Cheddar's inherent saltiness usually won't leave you wanting to salt this spread, so wait until the flavors have fully come together in the fridge for a few hours before making that call.

Charleston Cheese Ball

SERVES 10 TO 12

Pineapples have long symbolized Southern hospitality, but especially so in the sultry port city of Charleston, South Carolina. Its centuries-long business ties to the West Indies are reflected in its culinary history of serving tropically flavored—if not daringly bold—chutneys and curries to well-heeled, well-traveled people. Beau Monde, the Spice Islands brand's legendary seasoning, is an heirloom-exotic blend of salt, celery, and onion with an underlying sweetness (think cloves, allspice, nutmeg, and mace). You can tweak this cheese ball recipe any number of ways by using different cheeses, crumbled bacon, plumped golden raisins, or dried cranberries . . . you get the idea. Serve with hearty crackers.

1 pound cream cheese, at room temperature

½ cup mango chutney

⅓ cup finely sliced fresh chives or green onions

1 teaspoon Beau Monde or Old Bay Seasoning

1 cup shredded sharp white Cheddar cheese

½ cup finely chopped pecan pieces, toasted (see page 89), plus 2 to 2½ cups (about 120) unbroken, equally sized pecan halves, toasted

Salt

½ teaspoon curry powder (optional)

1 tablespoon orange-flavored liqueur (such as Cointreau; optional)

⅛ teaspoon cayenne pepper (optional)

Rosemary sprigs for garnish

In a stand mixer fitted with the paddle attachment, combine the cream cheese, chutney, chives, and Beau Monde and blend until smooth, 1 to 2 minutes. Add the Cheddar and chopped pecan pieces and mix until just blended. Season with salt, if necessary, and the curry, liqueur, and cayenne (if using).

Scoop the cheese mixture onto a plate lined with plastic wrap overhanging each side. Fold each side of the plastic wrap up to cover the cheese and use your hands to press the mixture into a teardrop shape (it will be soft). Refrigerate the cheese ball for 8 hours to let the flavors meld and texture bind.

Loosely unwrap the cheese ball and let it sit at room temperature about 20 minutes. With the tip of the oval facing downward, work from the bottom up to place pecan halves in overlapping tile fashion to mimic a pineapple's exterior; add rosemary sprigs for the "crown" before serving.

Can-Do Spirit
• • •

Old Bay Seasoning hails from Baltimore and was created in 1939 by German immigrant Gustav Brunn as the perfect spice-and-herb mix for accentuating, not overpowering, Chesapeake Bay blue crabs, scallops, clams, oysters, and other delicately flavored seafoods. On OldBay.com, modern-day owner McCormick & Co. attributes the seasoning's success to eighteen ingredients, but only lists (in this order) salt, celery seed, and "spices" that include red pepper, black pepper, and paprika. I doubt we'll learn the dozen or so other spices anytime soon.

Gifted Baked Brie

SERVES 6 TO 8

This Brie en croûte *(in a crust) is ooey-gooey fab, and gets gobbled up almost the instant it hits the serving table. If possible, serve it on a warming platter to keep it good and spreadable. Accompany with water crackers and green apple slices.*

Half a 17.3-ounce package puff pastry sheets, thawed, or one 8-ounce can refrigerated crescent dough

One 8-ounce round Brie cheese (see Cooking Note)

¼ cup fruit preserves (e.g., chunky fig, peach, apricot, or raspberry)

3 to 4 tablespoons almond slices, toasted (see page 89)

1 egg

1 tablespoon water or heavy cream

Preheat the oven to 400°F.

Unfold the pastry sheet on a lightly floured surface. Roll it out ever so slightly to ensure you have enough to completely cover the cheese. (However, you don't want it too thin or the filling will ooze out.)

Use a fork to pierce the Brie a number of times to allow the forthcoming preserves to sink in. Place the cheese in the center of the pastry sheet. Top the cheese with the preserves, followed by the almonds. Fold the pastry sheet up over the cheese, preserves, and almonds so that it's completely covering them.

Trim off any excess pastry and press the edges together to seal. (Use extra pastry scraps to create the top of the "package," perhaps as a bow or cut into small fall leaf shapes for placing here or there. This is especially helpful in covering thin areas of the pastry.)

In a small bowl, combine the egg and water and brush it over the top of the pastry.

Lightly coat a pie plate with baking spray and place the wrapped cheese in the center of the plate. (At this point, you can tightly wrap it in plastic wrap and refrigerate for up to 12 hours.)

Bake until the pastry is golden brown, 22 to 25 minutes. (The pastry may split open, but it'll be fine.) Turn off the oven and leave the cheese in for 5 to 10 minutes. Remove the cheese from the oven and let it stand for 15 minutes before serving, preferably on a warming platter.

Cooking Note

Don't trim off the top of the cheese rind or you'll have a guaranteed mess. It keeps the baked cheese's gooey interior from flowing lava-like from the pastry.

Queso Fundido, My Darling

SERVES 8; MAKES ABOUT 7 CUPS

Queso fundido means "molten cheese," which this is—molten cheese made glorious with roasted mild poblano peppers and feisty chorizo sausage, like a hot take on ye olde nine-layer dip. I like this with lots of lime wedges and good cold beer.

2 poblano peppers

8 ounces pork chorizo sausage, casings removed (see Cooking Note)

1 tablespoon olive oil

1 small yellow onion, finely diced

2 garlic cloves, minced

½ to 1 teaspoon ground cumin

2 large Roma tomatoes, diced

¼ cup all-purpose flour

1 cup pale Mexican lager (such as Tecate)

2 cups shredded sharp white Cheddar cheese

2½ cups shredded Monterey Jack cheese

1 cup shredded mozzarella cheese

2 tablespoons chopped fresh cilantro, plus more for garnish (optional)

Splash of heavy cream, half-and-half, or whole milk (optional)

Roast the poblano peppers on aluminum foil under the broiler or hold them with tongs over an open flame, turning until they're blistered and blackened on all sides, 7 to 9 minutes.

Seal the peppers in a large plastic zip-top bag or place them in a medium bowl covered tightly with plastic wrap and let them steam and soften for about 15 minutes. When cool enough to handle, use a paring knife to peel off the skin, trim the stem ends, and remove the seeds. Dice the poblanos and set aside.

Place paper towels atop a plate; set aside.

In a Dutch oven or deep heavy skillet over medium heat, cook the chorizo, breaking it up as it cooks, about 7 minutes. With a slotted spoon, transfer the crumbled sausage to drain on the prepared plate.

In the same pot, add the olive oil, onion, garlic, and cumin and cook over medium-low heat until the onion is tender, 6 to 8 minutes. Add the tomatoes and poblanos and cook, stirring occasionally, until most of the tomato juices have evaporated, 2 to 3 minutes. Sprinkle the flour over the tomato mixture and stir constantly for several minutes. Stir in the lager, increase the heat to medium-high, and stir often until the mixture reaches a boil.

Turn the heat to low and whisk in each of the cheeses, 1 cup at a time, until the mixture is smooth. Transfer it to a small fondue pot or slow cooker set to low. Sprinkle with the reserved chorizo and the cilantro. If desired, add the cream to make the mixture creamier and richer and garnish it with additional cilantro before serving.

Cooking Note

Fresh Mexican-style chorizo is a highly spiced pork sausage that can be found near other sausages sold at most supermarkets or at Mexican grocers. It's not to be confused with dried and cured Spanish-style chorizo sausage, which has a milder, sometimes sweeter flavor.

Goodly Ranch Dip

SERVES 10; MAKES ABOUT 1¼ CUPS

Homemade ranch dressing never disappoints, unlike many commercial products, which smack of preservatives. Once you get a basic ranch dressing/dip to your liking, try any number of flavor enhancers, like finely chopped jalapeño or lots of extra black pepper. Also consider substituting cilantro for parsley; lime juice for lemon; minced green onion or chives for onion powder (used here to keep the texture smooth); plain yogurt or mayonnaise for sour cream; minced shallot for garlic; etc. Serve this with sliced veggies or as a cooling dipping sauce for spicy lil' meat pies (see page 44) or chicken wings (see page 100).

1 cup sour cream, plus more
as needed

½ cup buttermilk

1 tablespoon freshly squeezed
lemon juice, plus lemon zest
for garnish

1 large garlic clove, minced

3 tablespoons chopped fresh
Italian flat-leaf parsley, plus
more for garnish

1 teaspoon minced fresh dill or
¼ to ⅓ teaspoon dried (optional)

¾ teaspoon salt

½ teaspoon onion powder

½ teaspoon ground black pepper

⅛ to ¼ teaspoon cayenne pepper
(optional)

In a pint jar or quart mixing bowl, combine the sour cream, buttermilk, and lemon juice. Shake or whisk to mix well.

Add the garlic, parsley, dill, salt, onion powder, black pepper, and cayenne (if using) and shake (or whisk) again until well combined. If using a bowl, transfer the dressing to a container with a lid.

Refrigerate for about 2 hours before serving. Taste the mixture to adjust the seasonings and the texture by adding more sour cream. (Store in an airtight container in the refrigerator for up to 1 week. Shake well before each use.) If pouring the dip into individual serving containers, garnish them with parsley or lemon zest, if desired.

Shake It, Baby
• • •

Glass canning jars with tight-fitting caps make delightfully pragmatic vessels. Use them to shake and rigorously combine your dips and dressings while beautifully seeing what they are, then easily transport the dressing and shake to mix again before serving directly from the jar.

Caramelized Sweet Onion Dip

SERVES 14 TO 16; MAKES ABOUT 3 CUPS

Cooking sweet onions like Vidalias and Texas 1015s long and slow brings out the richness of their earthy flavor by way of caramelization. Serve this with crackers, corn chip scoops, or sliced fresh vegetables.

2 tablespoons butter

2 sweet onions, chopped

1 teaspoon salt

½ teaspoon ground black pepper

One 16-ounce container regular or light sour cream

3 tablespoons finely sliced green onions or chives, plus finely sliced green onions or chives or chopped fresh parsley for garnish (optional)

Dash of Worcestershire sauce

In a large nonstick skillet over medium heat, melt the butter. Add the chopped onions, turn the heat to low, and cook, stirring occasionally, until the onions are soft and browned, about 25 minutes. Sprinkle the onions with ½ teaspoon of the salt and ¼ teaspoon of the pepper. Remove the pan from the heat and let stand 25 minutes to cool.

In a medium bowl, stir to combine the caramelized onions, sour cream, and 3 tablespoons green onions. Stir in the remaining ½ teaspoon salt, ¼ teaspoon pepper, and Worcestershire. Cover the onion spread and refrigerate it at least 1 hour (for best flavor), or up to 2 days. Garnish with sliced green onions, chives, or chopped fresh parsley, if desired, before serving.

Oysters Rockefeller Spinach Dip

SERVES 6; MAKES ABOUT 3 CUPS

This Southern party favorite hails from New Orleans native Katherine Fausset, a literary agent who lives in Brooklyn with her husband, who also happens to be from New Orleans—and also is a literary agent. The duo was introduced by a mutual friend who thought they'd have a lot in common. (Obviously they did.) A few years later, they were married at legendary French Quarter restaurant Arnaud's, which is owned by longtime friends of Katherine's family. This recipe, similar to the dish Arnaud's makes, was featured in Katherine's 2002 book, The Cooking Club Cookbook. *Katherine serves this in traditional fashion with Melba toast rounds.*

1 tablespoon olive oil

12 fresh oysters, shucked and drained

One 10-ounce package frozen chopped spinach, cooked and drained

4 ounces regular or light cream cheese, softened

½ cup grated Parmesan cheese

½ cup regular or light mayonnaise

½ cup regular or light sour cream

2 teaspoons freshly squeezed lemon juice

2 green onions, thinly sliced

1 garlic clove, pressed or minced

1 tablespoon Worcestershire sauce

½ teaspoon salt

10 drops Tabasco sauce

Ground black pepper

2 tablespoons Herbsaint or Pernod liqueur (optional)

Chopped fresh Italian flat-leaf parsley for garnish (optional)

Preheat the oven to 350°F.

In a large skillet over medium heat, warm the olive oil. Cook the oysters for about 5 minutes, or until their edges curl. Remove the pan from the heat. (And if necessary, cut any large oysters in two or three pieces.)

In a food processor or blender, combine the spinach, cream cheese, Parmesan, mayonnaise, sour cream, and lemon juice. Transfer the mixture to a bowl and stir in the green onions, garlic, Worcestershire, salt, and Tabasco. Season with pepper and add the Herbsaint, if desired. (At this point, you can cover the dip tightly and refrigerate for up to 1 day.)

Gently fold the oysters into the spinach mixture. Spoon the mixture into a small (about 3-cup) casserole or baking dish and bake until bubbly, about 25 minutes. Serve warm in a fondue pot or chafing dish, garnished with parsley, if desired.

Anise Amour
· · ·

Anise-flavored Herbsaint was created in 1934 by J. Marion Legendre and Reginald Parker of New Orleans, who'd learned how to make absinthe while in France during World War I. After Prohibition was repealed, they couldn't wait to put what they'd learned into practice (or better yet, into *bottles*). Eighty years later, their absinthe-inspired recipe has morphed into the liqueur we still love today—one similar to Pernod, invented two years earlier in France after absinthe was outlawed. (See Sources, page 138.)

Lemony Artichoke-Parmesan Spread

SERVES 10; MAKES ABOUT 4½ CUPS

It's amazing how much a sunny burst of lemon can so beautifully update the flavor and look of this party classic. Serve it warm with crostini (see page 81), pita chips, or gourmet crackers. Another idea? Spread the unbaked dip onto baguette slices and lightly broil until golden and bubbly.

Two 14-ounce cans artichoke hearts, drained and chopped

1¼ cups grated Parmesan cheese

¾ to 1 cup regular or light mayonnaise

1½ to 2 tablespoons freshly squeezed lemon juice, 1 teaspoon lemon zest, plus more zest for garnish (optional)

2 garlic cloves, minced

Preheat the oven to 350°F. Grease a 1- or 1½-quart baking dish.

Combine the artichoke hearts, 1 cup of the Parmesan, the mayonnaise, lemon juice, lemon zest, and garlic and spoon the mixture into the prepared baking dish. Sprinkle with the remaining ¼ cup Parmesan. (At this point, you can cover the dip tightly in plastic wrap and refrigerate for up to 1 day.)

Bake the dip uncovered until bubbly and lightly browned, about 30 minutes. Garnish with additional lemon zest, if desired, before serving.

Death by Mayonnaise

I cherish a sheet of paper sent to me by my late cousin, designer/cookbook author extraordinaire/Bunkie, Louisiana, native Lee Bailey. Emblazoned in bold newspaper type are the sardonic words "Death by Mayonnaise"—underneath which Lee has written, "The old ways are the best ways."

To that I say, "Hear, hear!" Or rather, "Here, here!" While we Southerners eat so much mayo we practically put it on our aspirin, most of it is meant to make smooth work of tomato aspics and shrimp salads and such.

A peek inside our grocery-store buggies and iceboxes would likely include the blue-ribboned label of Hellmann's, which many consider the best commercially available mayonnaise, one created in 1912 way up north in New York City.

"Up South" in the Carolinas and adjoining states, Duke's Mayonnaise has been a mainstay since 1917, and now claims a bit of a cult following around the country. I can see why; it *is* good, with a flavor very similar to homemade.

Creamy Collard Greens Spread

SERVES 12; MAKES ABOUT 3 CUPS

Enjoy a different take on spinach dip—one using collard greens, which have a beefier texture that won't wilt as much as spinach (yet have less bite than mustard or turnip greens). They're complemented here by smoky bacon and the earthy, nutty flavor of Gruyère cheese. Serve this spread with crostini (see page 81), crackers, or sticks of cornbread.

3 slices bacon

1 small sweet onion, finely chopped

1 medium red bell pepper, seeded and chopped

1 pound fresh collard greens, washed, trimmed, coarsely chopped (see Cooking Note)

2 or 3 garlic cloves, minced

¼ to ½ teaspoon pepper vinegar or hot sauce (optional)

One 8-ounce package regular or light cream cheese, cubed, softened

½ cup regular or light sour cream

¼ cup shredded Gruyère, Emmentaler, or smoked Swiss cheese

1 teaspoon Cajun seasoning

Preheat the oven to 350°F. Place paper towels on a plate and set it aside.

In a large skillet over medium heat, cook the bacon until crisp; drain the bacon on the prepared plate, leaving the drippings in the skillet.

Add the onion and bell pepper to the skillet. Cook over medium heat, stirring occasionally, until the vegetables are just tender, about 5 minutes. Add the collard greens, garlic, and vinegar (if using); cover and cook the mixture until tender, stirring occasionally, 10 to 12 minutes. Remove the pan from the heat.

Add the cream cheese, sour cream, Gruyère, and Cajun seasoning to the collard greens mixture, stirring to combine. Crumble the cooked bacon into the mixture, removing any fatty parts of the bacon, if desired. Spread the collards mixture into a 1½-quart casserole dish.

Bake, uncovered, until thoroughly heated, 10 to 12 minutes. Serve warm or at room temperature.

Cooking Note

Commercially bagged collard greens are pre-washed and trimmed, which is a major time-saver. To use a fresh bundle of greens, clean the leaves by soaking them, sometimes several times, in cool to lukewarm water. Use a wooden spoon to swirl them around to help dislodge any residual grit clinging to them, completely draining and cleaning the sink in between soaks. Once the leaves are clean, fold each one along the thick center rib, tearing away the leaves before discarding the tough stalks. Stack the leaves and coarsely cut them into 1-inch-wide pieces.

Divine Crab Spread

I know, I know, jumbo lump crab is practically sold by the carat, but if you really want to pamper your guests, treat them to this when you can. This go-to favorite was adapted from the winning recipe of the 1971 National Hard Crab Derby in Crisfield, Maryland. Here it's served delightfully cold, but it also can be served warm in a chafing dish. Offer it with Toasted Crostini (page 81), buttery crackers, celery ribs, sliced raw summer squash, or in pre-baked tartlet shells. Make sure the crab meat is kept very cold in the refrigerator by nestling the container in ice.

8 ounces whipped cream cheese

¼ cup heavy cream or half-and-half

¼ cup freshly squeezed lemon juice, ½ to 1 teaspoon lemon zest, plus thinly sliced lemon wedges for garnish

2 tablespoons chopped fresh chives or finely sliced green onions, plus whole chives for garnish

1 to 2 tablespoons mayonnaise

1 teaspoon Worcestershire sauce

¼ to ½ teaspoon salt

⅛ teaspoon hot sauce

1 pound jumbo lump crab meat, picked over for shells

In a medium bowl, combine the cream cheese, cream, lemon juice, lemon zest, chives, mayonnaise, Worcestershire, salt, and hot sauce and stir until smooth.

Gently add the crab meat, using a rubber spatula to fold it into the cream cheese mixture until just combined. Refrigerate the dip for at least 2 hours, or up to 1 day. To preserve the freshest flavor, keep the dip in a well-sealed container surrounded by ice in a larger container. Serve it very cold, garnished with lemon wedges and whole chives.

Cool Container

* * *

A large abalone shell makes a beautiful, see-worthy serving vessel for this. Line the base with just enough plastic wrap to keep the dip from escaping through the shell's small holes but also be hidden under the dip. (Doing this also will offer easier cleanup and insulate the food from any man-made coating that could be on the shell.)

Bourbony Chicken Liver Pâté

SERVES 10 TO 12; MAKES ABOUT 2 CUPS

Those who like chicken liver will find this mild, buttery, caramel-hued, bourbon-kissed spread nothing short of ravishing. If you can, wait three days before eating this to bring the flavors to their collective best. Once out of cold storage, let it sit at room temperature about 30 minutes to lose some of its frigidity. Serve with grilled or buttery Toasted Crostini (page 81) and hot-pepper jelly.

1 pound chicken livers

2 cups whole milk

½ cup bourbon

½ cup unsalted butter, cold

2 tablespoons minced shallots

1½ teaspoons minced fresh thyme

2 to 3 tablespoons heavy cream

2 tablespoons aged sherry vinegar (see Cooking Notes)

½ teaspoon salt

¼ teaspoon ground black pepper

⅛ teaspoon ground allspice

In a colander, rinse the livers to remove any bits of residue, and use kitchen shears or a knife to remove any excess fat or tissue. With a fork, prick holes in the livers (to allow for better absorption of flavors).

Add the prepared livers and milk to a medium bowl (adding a little more milk if necessary to ensure the livers are nearly submerged). Cover and refrigerate for at least 1 hour, or overnight (to produce a creamier, mellower flavor). Drain the livers and discard the milk. Pat the livers dry with paper towels.

In a small saucepan over medium heat, bring ⅓ cup of the bourbon to a boil. (Watch carefully, holding a tight-fitting lid; if the bourbon ignites, quickly cover the saucepan to tamp out the flame before removing the lid.) Cook until the liquid is reduced by half (you should have about 3 tablespoons), 3 to 4 minutes.

In a large skillet over medium heat, melt ¼ cup of the butter. (Keep the remaining butter cold until later use.) Add the shallots and sauté until tender and translucent, 3 to 4 minutes. Add the thyme and livers and cook, stirring occasionally to let the livers mingle with the other ingredients, until the livers are lightly browned and just-cooked on the inside (light pink but not raw, and not brown from overcooking), 5 to 7 minutes. Remove the mixture from the heat and let it cool slightly.

In the bowl of a food processor, combine the liver mixture with 2 tablespoons of the cream and gradually add the remaining $\frac{1}{4}$ cup butter, cut into small cubes. Once evenly puréed, blend in the remaining bourbon, the sherry vinegar, $\frac{1}{4}$ teaspoon of the salt, the pepper, and the allspice. Add the remaining 1 tablespoon cream and the remaining salt, if desired, and adjust the seasonings. Purée until it reaches the desired consistency. (If desired, press the liver mixture through a fine-mesh sieve into a medium bowl for the ultimate smoothness.)

Carefully pour or spoon the pâté into a 2- to 3-cup glass jar with a tight-fitting lid. Cover tightly and chill at least 24 hours, but preferably 2 days (the flavors will be good) to 3 days (it will be divine), before serving.

Cooking
Notes

Aged sherry vinegar gives this a rich and nutty flavor with only a touch of sweetness. A tablespoon of red wine vinegar plus a tablespoon of white wine vinegar is a fine substitute.

Leftovers can be kept in an airtight jar or container and refrigerated for about a week. To extend its life another week or so, add a thin coating of melted clarified butter on top, with a decorative sprig or two of thyme, to further seal in freshness once the lid is popped.

Lima Bean Hummus

Oh. My. Stars. Since learning how to make this, I've become addicted. Just wait. You'll see. Serve it with toasted wedges of pita bread or naan. (P.S.: Use the same two lemons to give you both the zest and the juice.)

One 16-ounce package frozen lima beans

1 cup extra-virgin olive oil

¼ cup tahini paste

2 or 3 garlic cloves

2 teaspoons lemon zest, plus more for garnish, plus 2 tablespoons freshly squeezed lemon juice

1 teaspoon sea salt

¼ teaspoon cayenne pepper

Paprika for garnish (optional)

In a medium saucepan, bring 1 cup water to a boil. Add the lima beans to the boiling water and, when the water returns to a boil, cover the pan, turn the heat to low, and cook the beans until they are just tender, 10 to 12 minutes. Drain the beans and let cool. Set aside 5 or 6 whole lima beans for garnish.

In the bowl of a food processor, combine ½ cup of the olive oil, the tahini paste, garlic, lemon zest, lemon juice, salt, and cayenne. Mix until blended. Add the cooked lima beans in small batches, slowly adding the remaining ½ cup oil (or more) and scraping down the sides of the bowl to ensure even blending, until the mixture is smooth and creamy. Garnish with the reserved beans, lemon zest, and paprika, if desired, before serving.

Chunky Guacamole

SERVES 8; MAKES ABOUT 4 CUPS

This is terrific when served with root-veggie chips (especially Sweet Potato Crisps, page 78) or Homemade Tortilla Chips (page 80). It serves a crowd of eight, so make only half of this for a smaller gathering.

5 or 6 ripe avocados

¼ cup chopped fresh cilantro, plus more for garnish (optional)

1 or 2 medium jalapeño peppers, seeded and minced

1 garlic clove, minced

¼ cup finely chopped red onion (optional)

3 or 4 Roma tomatoes (optional), seeded and chopped

2 to 3 tablespoons freshly squeezed lime juice

¾ teaspoon salt

Cut the avocados in half. Scoop the pulp into a bowl and dice it into small pieces or mash it with a fork or potato masher, as desired.

Gently fold in the cilantro, jalapeños, and garlic. Add the onion and tomatoes (if using). Stir in the lime juice and salt and adjust the seasonings. Cover the mixture with plastic wrap. (At this point, you can store it in the refrigerator for up to 6 hours.) Let it sit at room temperature for at least 30 minutes before serving. Garnish with additional cilantro, if desired.

No Brown, Please

Keep your guacamole from turning an icky shade of brown by placing a layer of plastic wrap directly on the mixture's surface. Keep the dip fresher looking and tastier by serving only half of it, replenishing it with fresh dip from the fridge as necessary.

Roasted Tomato Salsa

SERVES 10 TO 12; MAKES ABOUT 2¼ CUPS

After a number of pitiful goes at developing the freshest, most authentic-tasting, achingly beautiful salsa, I offer into evidence one that's as close to perfection as possible. Nearly everyone wants this recipe after having it, maybe because of its earthy depth from the roasted vegetables, with the jalapeño adding just the right amount of lift. This salsa goes well with everything without overpowering it. If you want more heat, add an extra roasted jalapeño. This also makes a nice food gift.

1 pound Roma tomatoes, sliced vertically

2 tomatillos, husked and sliced vertically

1 medium jalapeño pepper, seeded and sliced vertically

½ cup chopped yellow onion

½ cup chopped fresh cilantro

2 garlic cloves

1 to 1½ tablespoons freshly squeezed lime juice

1 tablespoon extra-virgin olive oil

1 tablespoon chopped fresh oregano or 1 teaspoon dried

1 teaspoon roasted or regular ground cumin

1 teaspoon chili powder

½ to 1 teaspoon salt (see Cooking Note)

¼ teaspoon ground black pepper

Place an oven rack in the position closest to the broiler and set the broiler on the lowest setting. Line a rimmed baking sheet with aluminum foil.

Place the tomatoes, tomatillos, and jalapeño cut-sides down on the prepared baking sheet. Broil the vegetables until they are bubbly and beginning to char, 4 to 5 minutes, then remove from the oven. Flip the vegetables and return them to broil for another 4 minutes.

In a food processor or blender, combine the roasted vegetables (watch it; they'll be hot to the touch), onion, cilantro, garlic, lime juice, olive oil, oregano, cumin, chili powder, salt, and pepper. Pulse until the mixture reaches the desired consistency, scraping down the sides to evenly blend.

Pour the salsa into a storage container, loosely cover with plastic wrap, and let it sit at room temperature for about 30 minutes before adding a tight-fitting cover. Refrigerate for at least 4 hours, but preferably overnight, or up to 5 days. Adjust the seasonings as desired after the flavors have properly united before serving.

Cooking Note

I give a range for the salt here, but you may find yourself, as I did, adding the other ½ teaspoon once the salsa's flavors have melded. The vegetables seem to drink it in better, given time. You may want to add only ¼ teaspoon more or none at all; that's your call.

Strawberry-Beet Salsa

This takes a bit of chopping work, but it's a sparkling showstopper—especially served atop vibrant Sweet Potato Crisps (page 78) or tucked into endive leaves. Use any leftover salsa on seared fish or grilled chicken or pork.

8 ounces peeled, steamed baby red beets (see Cooking Note)

8 ounces hulled, ripe, fresh strawberries

3 tablespoons finely chopped red onion

3 tablespoons finely chopped fresh cilantro

1½ teaspoons honey

2 teaspoons freshly squeezed lime juice

¼ to ½ teaspoon hot sauce (optional)

Salt (optional)

Finely chop the beets and strawberries and add them to a large bowl.

Stir in the onion, cilantro, honey, and lime juice. Add the hot sauce (if using) and season with salt, if necessary. Refrigerate, well covered, for about 2 hours before serving.

Cooking Note

To save time, I buy steamed baby beets available from large or specialty supermarkets (I especially like ones packaged by Trader Joe's or Melissa's; see Sources, page 138). In a pinch, well-drained canned beets will work fine. To steam them at home, place peeled, trimmed baby beets in a steamer rack fitted within a pot of 2 or 3 inches of boiling water; cover and cook for 7 to 10 minutes, until they are fork-tender. Remove the beets and allow them to cool before dicing.

Shrimp Butter

It's called shrimp butter for its creamy consistency, which makes a nice contrast to the more gelatinous version of this iconic seafood spread. A fleur de lis–shaped baking pan or mold makes a lovely, festive cradle for it. Serve with good-quality crackers.

1½ pounds large Perfectly Boiled Shrimp (see page 77), peeled

One 8-ounce package cream cheese, softened

½ cup mayonnaise

2 green onions, finely chopped

2 teaspoons Dijon mustard

¼ to ½ teaspoon Old Bay or Cajun seasoning

Paprika for seasoning (optional)

Dash of hot sauce (optional)

Dash of ground black pepper (optional)

Chopped fresh Italian flat-leaf parsley and lemon slices for garnish (optional)

Place the shrimp in a food processor and pulse eight to ten times, until the shrimp are finely chopped but not mushy.

In a medium bowl, stir to combine the cream cheese, mayonnaise, green onions, mustard, and Old Bay; fold in the chopped shrimp. Adjust the seasonings with paprika, hot sauce, and black pepper, if desired.

Line a 2-cup mold or glass bowl with plastic wrap, leaving lots of overhang. Place the shrimp mixture into the mold, packing it tightly with a spatula. Cover it with the plastic wrap overhang and chill in the refrigerator for at least 3 hours, or up to 2 days.

Unwrap the plastic overhang and invert the mold onto a plate. Remove the rest of the plastic wrap. Garnish with chopped parsley and lemon slices, if desired. Let the spread sit for at least 15 minutes at room temperature before serving.

Tequila-Spiked Cocktail Sauce with Perfectly Boiled Shrimp

SERVES 4, FIVE OR SIX SHRIMP EACH; MAKES 2 CUPS SAUCE

Tequila helps amplify the sprightly ingredients of a classic cocktail sauce, but do use a smooth, superior-quality one (blanco, reposado, or añejo) or the (potentially bitter) flavor could disappoint. To make sure this sauce and its boiled shrimp partner stay their fresh-best, unless you're serving the shrimp hot (to be eaten immediately), keep them very cold in bowls surrounded by ice. Serving them directly atop a bed of ice invariably leads people to plunge their hands into the frigid water to fish them out, and the shrimp can become shriveled and rubbery. Leave their tail shells on if you plan to serve them "cocktail" style—via sherry glasses, champagne coupes, or small martini glasses with a bit of sauce atop a little shredded lettuce.

TEQUILA-SPIKED COCKTAIL SAUCE

One 12-ounce bottle chili sauce

¼ cup good tequila

2 tablespoons prepared horseradish (see headnote, page 35)

1½ tablespoons chopped fresh cilantro

1 tablespoon freshly squeezed lime or lemon juice, plus 1 teaspoon lime or lemon zest

1 teaspoon hot sauce

PERFECTLY BOILED SHRIMP

1 small lemon, quartered

2 tablespoons dried seafood boil seasoning, or one 3-ounce boil-in-bag seasoning mix (for both I like Zatarain's; see Sources, page 138)

1½ pounds large (21/25 count) shrimp, unpeeled

Lime slices or wedges for garnish (optional)

To make the cocktail sauce: In a small bowl, stir to combine the chili sauce, tequila, horseradish, cilantro, lime juice, lime zest, and hot sauce. Cover and refrigerate about 1 hour before serving to let the flavors meld. (Store in an airtight container in the refrigerator for up to 3 days.)

To make the shrimp: Add 1 quart water to a Dutch oven or small stockpot. Squeeze in the lemon juice and drop the lemon quarters into the water. Stir in the seafood boil seasoning and bring the ingredients to a boil.

Add the shrimp and cook just until they turn pink, about 2 minutes. Drain and rinse with cold water.

Stir the cocktail sauce well before serving it with the shrimp, peeled and deveined or in their shells. Garnish with lime slices or wedges, if desired.

Sweet Potato Crisps

SERVES 8 TO 10

A mandoline set at the thinnest level will make quick work of slicing a sweet potato, but it'll take some patience to cook your way through the towering mound of slices. The results will be rewarding, though, for the effort involved. I don't advise baking them if you plan to serve the chips with dips and spreads; they tend to shrivel up, leaving very little surface. Don't bother to peel them first if you're slicing them thinly; the fine ring of skin gives them character. If serving these without a dip, consider sprinkling on some fresh lime juice and rosemary-infused sea salt. These chips are exceptional with salsas, guacamole, and sweet onion dip.

1 large sweet potato, 2½ to 3 inches at widest

Vegetable oil for frying

Coarse sea salt

Wash the sweet potato and pat it dry. Use a mandoline or other V-blade slicer to cut the sweet potato into very thin slices ($\frac{1}{16}$ to $\frac{1}{8}$ inch thick).

Pour vegetable oil to a depth of several inches in an electric fryer or deep, heavy-duty skillet outfitted with a fry/candy thermometer. Heat the oil to 350°F. Line a plate with paper towels.

Fry the potato slices in batches of five or six until golden and beginning to bubble and "hiss," 2 to 3 minutes. Remove the chips with a slotted spoon and drain on the prepared plate. Sprinkle lightly with coarse salt.

Store in an airtight container at room temperature for up to 2 days.

Homemade Tortilla Chips

SERVES 8 TO 10

Okay, you can *bake these (see Cooking Note), but they won't have the rich texture and flavor that your guests will love having in fried form. They are especially good with salsas, guacamole, and warm, cheesy dips.*

Vegetable oil for frying

Ten 6-inch corn tortillas

1 tablespoon freshly squeezed lime juice (optional)

Coarse sea salt (optional)

All-purpose Mexican seasoning (optional)

Pour vegetable oil to a depth of several inches in an electric fryer or deep, heavy-duty skillet outfitted with a fry/candy thermometer. Heat the oil to 350°F. Line a plate with paper towels.

Stack the tortillas and cut them into sixths. Fry the tortilla wedges in the hot oil in small batches until crisp and golden, about 1 minute, turning midway through. Drain on the prepared plate and season with the lime juice, salt, and/or Mexican seasoning, if desired.

Store in an airtight container at room temperature for up to 2 days.

Cooking Note

To bake these, preheat the oven to 350°F. Lay out the tortilla wedges on a rimmed baking pan and brush with 2 tablespoons olive oil. Bake until crisp, about 7 minutes, turning halfway through the cooking time if the chips darken faster than expected. Season as desired.

Toasted Crostini

SERVES 8, ABOUT FOUR CROSTINI EACH

This is an easy-to-make must-have to serve with nearly any cold or warm spread.
Use good-quality bread.

1 French baguette

2 to 3 tablespoons extra-virgin olive oil or melted butter

Coarse sea salt (optional)

Preheat the oven to 400°F.

Slice the baguette into $\frac{1}{4}$-inch-thick slices on the diagonal. Line a large rimmed baking sheet with close-fitting rows of bread and brush or drizzle them lightly with the olive oil. Sprinkle with salt if you think necessary (but consider what may be spread atop each slice).

Bake for 6 to 8 minutes, or until lightly browned. Cool on a wire rack about 3 minutes.

Store in an airtight container at room temperature for up to 2 days.

Cornbread Blinis

These small cornmeal "pancakes" are beautiful, sturdy hosts for the likes of thinly sliced prosciutto or smoked salmon with creamy herbed cheese or a flavored mayo.

½ cup good-quality stone-ground yellow cornmeal (see Sources, page 138)

½ cup all-purpose flour

3 tablespoons sugar

1 teaspoon baking powder

½ teaspoon salt

½ cup milk

1 egg, lightly beaten

4 tablespoons butter; 2 tablespoons melted

2 to 3 tablespoons finely chopped fresh chives or Italian flat-leaf parsley (optional)

In a medium bowl, whisk to combine the cornmeal, flour, sugar, baking powder, and salt. Whisk in the milk, beaten egg, melted butter, and chives (if using). Stir until just combined.

Heat 1 tablespoon butter in a hot skillet or griddle. When bubbly, add batter in tablespoonfuls about 1 inch apart. Cook the blinis until bubbles form on top, about 2 minutes. Flip and cook another minute or so, until lightly browned and golden. Remove them to a cooling rack and, if desired, keep warm in an oven heated to its lowest temperature. Use paper towels to wipe away crust giblets or darkened grease from the pan. Repeat the process with more butter and batter.

Store in an airtight container in the refrigerator for up to 3 days, or in the freezer for up to 1 month.

CHAPTER FOUR

SIT FOR A SPELL:
Reach for a Chair and Utensil

....

These are the dishy delectables requiring a knife, fork, or spoon—and at times your full attention—since they're covered in sauces you'd prefer to eat rather than wear.

These appetizers—say, a gracious, classic aspic or sprightly strawberry salad with bourbon vinaigrette—whet appetites before a grand lunch or dinner. They can also provide more substantial sustenance, as with layered cornbread salad in a jar or jerk-seasoned riblets.

In sum, these hors d'oeuvres are best enjoyed with the proper seating and surface to savor the fare in relaxing style, be it at an intimate gathering or large-scale dinner.

Tomato Aspic

SERVES 12

*Congealed tomato salad: Who could ask for anything more? (I'm serious!) This recipe,
inspired by The Carriage House restaurant in my hometown of Natchez, Mississippi, makes
cool little aspics stuffed with a bit of cream cheese and topped with mayonnaise for true
respite on sweltering days. (For a "Blossom" mold, see Sources, page 138.)*

½ cup boiling water

Two 0.25-ounce envelopes
unflavored gelatin

3 cups thick tomato juice, warmed

1 small onion, very finely minced

2 ribs celery, very finely minced

1 tablespoon freshly squeezed
lemon juice, plus lemon zest
for garnish

2 teaspoons Worcestershire sauce

1 teaspoon salt

½ teaspoon ground black pepper

½ teaspoon Tabasco sauce

8 ounces whipped cream cheese
(whipped cream cheese will offer
a softer interior texture)

Spring or Butter lettuce mix
for serving

Good-quality mayonnaise
for serving

Chopped toasted pecans
for garnish

Pour the boiling water into a medium bowl and sprinkle the gelatin over it. When the gelatin is completely dissolved, stir in the tomato juice, making sure all the lumps are gone; if they persist, reheat the mixture briefly. Stir in the onion, celery, lemon juice, Worcestershire, salt, pepper, and Tabasco and let cool slightly.

Use a melon scoop or tablespoon to make twelve 1-inch-diameter balls of whipped cream cheese; place on a small plate and refrigerate until ready for use.

Pour the tomato mixture in twelve ¹/₂-cup molds (two 6-cavity silicone mold trays are ideal) and refrigerate for 1 hour before adding the cream cheese (the gelatin mixture should be slightly set or the balls will sink to the bottom of each cavity and disrupt the mold's pattern). Carefully insert the balls of whipped cream cheese just until submerged (avoid pressing too far down or you may disrupt the mold's exterior pattern). Refrigerate for 12 to 24 hours to ensure the aspic is well set.

Before serving, run a knife around the top edge of each mold and set it in a shallow bowl of hot water just long enough to loosen the gelatin. (If using a silicone mold, place it on a cutting board and top with an inverted serving platter; press down securely before inverting to unmold.) Refrigerate the aspics again to ensure they stay cold and set.

Add a handful of small lettuce leaves to each salad plate, top with an aspic, put a dab of mayonnaise on each, and garnish with the lemon zest and pecans to serve.

Minted Watermelon & Feta Salad

SERVES 8 TO 10

The make-ahead element to this exquisite salty-sweet-cool salad is just prepping the ingredients and chilling them until showtime. Toss everything just before you eat to keep it all looking, and tasting, its best. This version has feta, but for slightly bolder flavor try mild blue cheese. And while "seedless" watermelon does have some seeds, they're soft, white, and okay to eat—plus pretty to look at.

One 4-pound seedless watermelon

1 medium sweet onion

1 bunch fresh spearmint

½ to ¾ cup white balsamic vinegar or red wine vinegar

¼ to ½ teaspoon salt

¼ teaspoon ground black pepper

¼ to ½ cup grapeseed oil or extra-virgin olive oil

6 ounces feta cheese, crumbled

Slice the watermelon and cut away the fruity flesh. Cut the fruit into bite-size pieces. Place them in a large plastic zip-top bag or bowl tightly covered with plastic wrap and refrigerate for up to 1 day.

Peel and thinly slice the sweet onion into rings. Place them in a medium zip-top plastic bag or bowl fitted with plastic wrap and refrigerate for up to 1 day.

Identify small unblemished leaves and full leafy sections from the mint. Pluck away smaller leaves for sprinkling onto the salad as is; set aside. Chop the larger leaves into smaller pieces; set aside. You'll want about ¼ cup total. Reserve 8 to 10 small sprigs for garnishes, if desired.

Place the mint leaves, chopped mint, and mint sprigs within the folds of several paper towels that have been rinsed with cool water and drained slightly. Place the mint, loosely covered, in plastic zip-top bags and refrigerate for up to 2 hours.

In a pint-size canning jar, combine the vinegar, salt, and pepper. Put on the lid and shake the jar until the ingredients are well mixed. Uncover and very slowly whisk in the grapeseed oil. Add the chopped mint. Shake, taste, and adjust the seasonings as needed. Once the flavor is to your liking, seal the jar and shake it once more for good measure. Refrigerate it for at least 2 hours to let the flavors meld, or for up to 2 days.

Reshake the dressing and set it aside for 20 minutes. Fill eight to ten small bowls two-thirds full with watermelon and add ⅛ cup each of onion and crumbled feta. Add the room-temperature dressing and mint leaves. Garnish with mint sprigs before serving.

Spinach Salad with Strawberries, Bacon, Blue Cheese & Bourbon Vinaigrette

SERVES 8 TO 10

This lovely spinach salad is both sweetened and spiked with bourbon vinaigrette. It's easy as pie to make and nice to serve to a crowd.

½ cup bourbon

1½ cups olive oil

¼ cup apple cider vinegar

2 tablespoons maple syrup

½ teaspoon sea salt

1 teaspoon ground black pepper

1 pound sliced bacon, chopped into small pieces

1 pound fresh spinach, washed and dried

1 pound hulled, ripe, fresh strawberries, sliced

1 cup pecan halves, toasted

2 green apples, diced

2 breakfast radishes, thinly sliced

8 ounces mild blue cheese, crumbled

In a small saucepan over medium heat, bring the bourbon to a boil. (Watch carefully, holding a tight-fitting lid; if the bourbon ignites, quickly cover the saucepan to tamp out the flame before removing the lid.) Cook until the liquid is reduced to about 2 tablespoons, 3 to 4 minutes. Transfer the reduction to a ramekin, cover with plastic wrap, and refrigerate it until well chilled.

In a small bowl, whisk to combine the olive oil, vinegar, maple syrup, salt, pepper, and reduced bourbon. Set the vinaigrette aside (or cover and refrigerate for up to 3 days).

Place several paper towels on a plate or paper bag; set aside.

In a medium skillet over medium-low heat, cook the bacon until crisp, 5 to 6 minutes. Transfer to the paper towel–lined plate to drain.

In a large bowl, combine the spinach, strawberries, pecans, apples, radishes, blue cheese, and cooked bacon. Toss gently with the vinaigrette and serve.

A Toast to Nuts

• • •

Warmed nuts amount to more flavorful nuts. Spread them evenly on a rimmed pan and bake at 350°F for 5 to 7 minutes, shaking them in the pan and/or turning them with a spatula halfway through cooking. When you start smelling them, they're ready (and can burn in an instant). Let them cool before handling.

Jars o' Cornbread Salad

SERVES 6

Pint-size layered cornbread salads will be the star of any barbecue, picnic, or tailgate thanks to their see-through culinary charm, portability, and style.

One 8.5-ounce box cornbread mix
(see Cooking Notes)

One 15-ounce can black beans,
rinsed and drained

One 15-ounce can
whole kernel corn with red and
green peppers, drained

6 Roma tomatoes,
cut into small dice

½ teaspoon lime zest, plus
2 tablespoons freshly squeezed
lime juice

1 teaspoon adobo with cumin
seasoning (see Cooking Notes)

7 slices bacon, cooked
and crumbled

2 cups shredded Mexican
cheese blend

⅓ cup finely chopped green onions

2 cups shredded lettuce

1 recipe Goodly Ranch Dip (page 58)
or one 0.4-ounce envelope
buttermilk ranch salad dressing
mix, prepared as directed (see
Cooking Notes)

Make the cornbread according to the package directions. Let it cool and crumble it into a large plastic zip-top storage bag or airtight plastic container. (This can be done a day or two in advance; keep it sealed airtight.)

In a medium bowl, add the black beans, corn with peppers, chopped tomatoes, lime zest, lime juice, and adobo with cumin seasoning; stir to combine. Let the salad marinate about 30 minutes. (This can be made a day or two in advance and kept refrigerated in an airtight container.)

In each of six wide-mouth pint-size glass canning jars, add $1\frac{1}{2}$ to 2 tablespoons cornbread crumbles, $1\frac{1}{2}$ teaspoons bacon, 1 table-spoon cheese blend, $1\frac{1}{2}$ teaspoons green onions, 3 tablespoons seasoned bean salad, a heaping 2 tablespoons lettuce, and 1 table-spoon ranch dip. Slightly press down each layer with the back of a small ($\frac{1}{4}$-cup) measuring cup or a spoon.

Repeat the layers to fill the jars. Cover and refrigerate the salads at least 1 hour, or up to 4 hours, before serving. (If stored longer, the mixture will get mushy.)

Cooking
Notes

The cornbread mix (e.g., Jiffy) will call for egg and milk; the dressing packet will require mayonnaise and buttermilk.

Adobo with cumin seasoning is a Mexican all-purpose seasoning blend; I like the one made by Goya (see Sources, page 138). To substitute, use $\frac{1}{4}$ teaspoon salt, $\frac{1}{4}$ teaspoon garlic powder, and $\frac{1}{2}$ teaspoon ground cumin.

Fresh Corn Cakes with Field Pea Relish & Lemon Aioli

SERVES 6 TO 8, TWO CORNCAKES EACH; MAKES 4 CUPS RELISH, 1 CUP AIOLI

Griddled corn cakes are colorful in both flavor and appearance, with the pea relish and garlicky, lemony mayo offering a zesty bonding experience. (Also try the relish with the Sweet Potato Crisps on page 78.) The beauty of this recipe is the freshness of the peas, but if necessary you can use frozen or well-rinsed and drained canned. Stone-ground cornmeal is available in most large grocery stores and specialty markets. For sources, see page 138.

FIELD PEA RELISH

3 cups water

1 cup low-sodium chicken broth

2¼ teaspoons salt

3 cups mixed fresh field peas (such as crowder, zipper, or lady)

⅓ cup canola or vegetable oil

⅓ cup freshly squeezed lime juice

¼ cup chopped fresh cilantro

1 tablespoon minced shallot

¼ teaspoon hot sauce

½ cup diced red onion

½ cup diced red bell pepper

LEMON AIOLI

1 cup good mayonnaise

1 teaspoon lemon zest, plus 3 tablespoons freshly squeezed lemon juice

1½ to 2 teaspoons minced garlic

¼ teaspoon ground black pepper

Salt

To make the relish: In a medium saucepan over high heat, bring the water and chicken broth (or enough of either to equal 4 cups) with 2 teaspoons of the salt to a boil. Add the peas and, when the water returns to a boil, turn the heat to medium and simmer the peas until just tender, 7 to 10 minutes. Drain the cooked peas in a colander and rinse them under cold water. Let cool and shake out any remaining water. Set aside.

In a large bowl, whisk to combine the canola oil, lime juice, cilantro, shallot, hot sauce, and remaining ¼ teaspoon salt. Add the cooled field peas, red onion, and red bell pepper, using a spatula to gently combine. (Cover and refrigerate for up to 2 days.)

To make the aioli: In a small bowl, stir together the mayonnaise, lemon zest, lemon juice, garlic, pepper, and ¼ teaspoon salt. Season with more salt if desired. Refrigerate in an airtight container for about 1 hour to ensure the flavors coalesce.

To make the corn cakes: In a small bowl, whisk to combine the egg and half-and-half.

In a large bowl, stir to combine the cornmeal, flour, baking powder, baking soda, and salt. Stir in the egg mixture, corn, and finely sliced green onion until just combined.

In a large skillet, heat 1 tablespoon of the butter over medium heat. Scoop two or three ¼-cup portions of batter into the pan.

Continued

FRESH CORN CAKES

1 egg, lightly beaten

1 cup half-and-half or milk

¾ cup stone-ground cornmeal

½ cup all-purpose flour

1¼ teaspoons baking powder

¾ teaspoon baking soda

½ teaspoon salt

3 cups fresh or frozen and thawed corn kernels

½ green onion, finely sliced

8 tablespoons butter or olive oil

Thinly sliced green onions, cut on the bias, for garnish (optional)

Cook the corn cakes for 3 to 4 minutes, or until the bottom of each cake is lightly browned and can hold its shape while being flipped. Cook for an additional minute, or until cooked through. Remove the cakes to a wire rack inserted into a baking pan and keep warm in the oven set at the lowest setting (they are good at room temperature too). Repeat the cooking process with the remaining butter and batter.

Place two corn cakes on each plate. Add ⅓ to ½ cup of the field pea relish. Dollop with the lemon aioli. Garnish with the sliced green onions, if desired, before serving.

Herbed Goat Cheese & Tomato Tarts

SERVES 8

Let guests brighten up these crispy, creamy, tangy summer lovelies with extra sprinkles of basil chiffonade (see page 112) and chopped chives (and brighten up themselves after the first bite). The extra pastry sheets in this recipe allow for the tarts' twisted borders, but also can be used to make edgings of small cut-outs of fall leaves, stars, hearts, or the like. Oh, and another thing—instead of each pastry sheet making four larger tarts, you can quarter them to make sixteen smaller pick-me-ups.

4 puff pastry sheets
(from two 17.3-ounce boxes),
thawed (see Cooking Note)

2 egg yolks, beaten with
2 tablespoons water

6 ounces herbed or regular goat
cheese, softened

3 tablespoons minced fresh basil,
plus 1 tablespoon basil chiffonade
for garnish (optional)

2 garlic cloves, pressed

2 tablespoons half-and-half or milk

1 teaspoon lemon zest, plus
2 teaspoons freshly squeezed
lemon juice

Sea salt (optional)

Ground black pepper (optional)

24 to 28 multicolored grape or
cherry tomatoes, halved

1½ tablespoons minced fresh
chives, plus more for garnish
(optional)

Preheat the oven to 400°F. Line two rimmed baking sheets with parchment paper or silicone baking mats; set aside.

Stacking two puff pastry sheets, make two cuts to create four even squares per sheet, or eight total.

Using the remaining stack of two pastry sheets, make seven cuts to create eight horizontal slices. Make a vertical cut down the center of the stack to create sixteen rectangular slices per sheet, or thirty-two total.

For each tart, make side "twists" by cutting the thirty-two rectangular strips in half horizontally, making sixty-four small strips. Weave each of two strips together to form thirty-two twisted strands.

Attach a dough twist on each side of the eight pastry squares, tucking in or trimming the overhanging dough so that it fits evenly and snugly. Place the squares on the baking sheets at least 2 inches apart.

Use a fork to prick holes into each tart square (this will help keep it from rising). Add pie weights, if desired. Use a pastry brush to paint the beaten egg onto the braided sides of each pastry square.

Bake the braided squares until puffy and lightly golden, about 15 minutes. (Store on a wire rack loosely covered with plastic wrap at room temperature for up to 4 hours.)

Continued

In a small bowl, use a fork to combine the goat cheese, minced basil, garlic, half-and-half, lemon zest, and lemon juice. Stir until creamy. Test for flavor and adjust the seasonings, adding a small amount of salt and pepper, if desired, and set aside.

Let the pastry cool for a couple of minutes before carefully removing the (hot) pie weights and pressing down any puffy sections.

Use a small rubber spatula to spread the herbed cheese mixture within each tart shell. Decoratively place the small tomato halves atop the cheese mixture. Sprinkle the chives across the top.

If desired, return the tarts to the oven and bake until the cheese is melted and slightly bubbly, about 5 minutes. Remove from the oven and let cool for 1 to 2 minutes.

Garnish each pastry with additional chives and basil chiffonade, if desired, before serving.

| Cooking Note | *Let frozen puff pastry thaw overnight in the refrigerator or at room temperature for about 30 minutes. Once unwrapped, on a lightly floured surface, brush the seams with a little water and press it together slightly with your fingers. Try not to handle the dough too much or it'll toughen up.* |

Chicken Tortilla Soup

SERVES 8

This light but rich-tasting, soul-comforting soup won't anchor your ship after you eat it, so you can easily set sail for other dishes on the party horizon. Serve it in small bowls, mugs, or mini kettles with Homemade Tortilla Chips (page 80) or perhaps rolled hot, small corn tortillas or cornbread sticks with butter and lime wedges.

1 tablespoon vegetable oil

1 medium yellow onion, thinly sliced

2 garlic cloves, minced

2 tablespoons minced fresh cilantro, plus more for garnish

1½ cups seeded and diced Roma tomatoes

1 teaspoon ground cumin

1½ teaspoons chili powder

4 cups chicken broth

Six 6-inch corn tortillas, cut into thin strips

Salt

1 to 2 boneless, skinless chicken breasts, cut into bite-size pieces, or 2 cups shredded cooked deli chicken

Ground black pepper

Sour cream, diced avocado, and grated Mexican-style cheese blend for topping (optional)

In a medium skillet over medium heat, warm the vegetable oil. Add the onion and garlic and sauté until just tender. Add the cilantro and continue to sauté 1 to 2 minutes more. Add this mixture to the bowl of a food processor fitted with the chopping blade, along with the tomatoes, and purée until smooth.

Transfer the tomato mixture back to the skillet and stir in the cumin and chili powder. Cook about 5 minutes more, or until the mixture becomes thickened and darkens in color; stir frequently. Transfer the mixture to a large pot and add the chicken broth. Cover and simmer about 20 minutes, stirring occasionally.

Preheat the oven to 400°F. Lightly coat a baking sheet with cooking spray.

Place the tortilla strips on the prepared baking sheet, spritz them evenly with cooking spray, and sprinkle with salt. Bake for 10 to 15 minutes, or until crisp, stirring occasionally. Remove from the sheet to cool. (Store in an airtight container for up to 2 days; reheat to crisp before serving, if desired.)

Add the chicken to the pot and simmer until it is cooked through (opaque throughout). Season the soup with salt and pepper. (At this point, you can let the soup cool and refrigerate it in an airtight container for up to 1 day. Reheat before serving.)

Ladle the soup into bowls and serve. Offer small bowls of the tortilla strips, cilantro, sour cream, avocado, and cheese, to top as desired.

Rum 'n' Coke Wings

SERVES 6 TO 8

Keep lots of napkins on hand for these wonderfully sticky glazed wings with a hint of tropical spice and "Co-cola" sweetness. (Hey, if we can use Coke in our cakes and barbecue sauces, we can use them in our chicken wing marinades, too.) If desired, serve this with Goodly Ranch Dip (page 58) or blue cheese dressing alongside celery ribs and carrot sticks.

3 pounds fresh or frozen, thawed chicken wings

Two 0.7-ounce packets taco seasoning

¼ to ⅓ cup olive oil

¼ cup butter

1 cup Coca-Cola

½ cup light rum

¼ cup mild hot sauce (e.g., Crystal, Frank's, Texas Pete, Tabasco)

2 tablespoons light honey

¼ cup finely chopped green onions (optional)

Preheat the oven to 450°F. Line a large, rimmed baking sheet with lightly greased heavy-duty aluminum foil.

Cut off the tips from the chicken wings and discard them; cut the wings in half at the joint, if desired. Rinse them and pat dry.

Empty the contents of one taco seasoning packet into a large, heavy-duty zip-top plastic bag. Add the wings and shake to coat. (You might have to do this in two batches.)

Place the lightly seasoned wings in a single layer on the prepared baking sheet. Drizzle with the olive oil and toss to completely coat with oil.

Bake the wings for about 45 minutes, or until browned and a thermometer inserted into the meat registers 165°F.

Lower the oven temperature to 350°F.

While the wings are baking, in a medium saucepan over medium-high heat, melt the butter. Whisk in the contents of the remaining taco seasoning packet, the cola, rum, hot sauce, and honey. Bring the mixture to a boil. (Watch carefully, holding a tight-fitting lid; if the rum ignites, quickly cover the saucepan to tamp out the flame before removing the lid.)

Turn the heat to low and cook until the mixture reaches a sticky glaze consistency capable of coating the back of a spoon, about 30 minutes.

Transfer the wings from the oven to a large bowl; discard the baking sheet's foil and drain off the residual oil.

Pour the rum-cola glaze over the wings. Cover the bowl and give it a few good shakes or use tongs to toss the wings. (At this point, you can place the wings in one or two heavy-duty plastic zip-top bags or other airtight container and refrigerate for up to 3 hours; the glaze will congeal but it will loosen up when baked.)

Add a new sheet of heavy-duty aluminum foil to the baking sheet and use tongs to place the glazed wings in a single layer. Bake the wings for 7 to 9 minutes to allow the glaze and the wings to commingle. Remove the glazed wings from the oven and serve them hot, garnished with the chopped green onions, if desired.

Brandied Baked Ham with Mustard Butter

SERVES 16 TO 20; MAKES ABOUT 2 CUPS MUSTARD BUTTER

Tea sandwiches (see page 47) are fashionable for daintier affairs, but for luncheons and the like, rely on stacks of tender sweet ham, soft biscuits, and mustard butter. Here, brandy infuses ham with aromatic elegance enhanced by the liquor's fruity overtones. Refined creamy mustard nicely balances a ham's sweetness. You serve thinly sliced ham sandwiched in soft biscuits or rolls with the mustard butter on the side.

BRANDIED BAKED HAM

1½ cups packed dark brown sugar

¼ cup brandy

2 tablespoons grainy mustard

One 5-pound bone-in half ham, fully cooked

1½ teaspoons whole cloves

MUSTARD BUTTER

2 cups butter, softened

¼ cup grated sweet onion

¼ cup Dijon or Creole mustard

To make the ham: In a small saucepan, stir to combine the brown sugar, brandy, and mustard. Bring the mixture to a boil over medium-high heat and, stirring constantly, cook until the glaze is thick and syrupy, about 3 minutes. (Watch carefully, holding a tight-fitting lid; if the brandy ignites, quickly cover the saucepan to tamp out the flame before removing the lid. Store in an airtight container in the refrigerator for up to 2 days. Reheat just before serving.)

Preheat the oven to 325°F. Line a shallow roasting pan with heavy-duty aluminum foil and place a wire rack on top.

Score the fat on top of the ham by making diagonal cuts in a diamond pattern. Insert the cloves into the intersections of each diamond. Place the ham on the rack in the prepared pan. Insert a meat thermometer, making sure it doesn't touch the bone.

Bake the ham for about 1 hour, or until the meat thermometer registers 125°F.

Remove the ham and brush on the brandy glaze. Return the ham to the oven and cook for 20 to 30 minutes more, or until the meat thermometer registers 135°F. Let it stand for 15 minutes. (The meat temperature will rise to 140°F.)

To make the mustard butter: In a medium bowl, stir to combine the butter, sweet onion, and mustard. Scrape it into a serving bowl.

Cut the ham into thin slices and arrange them on a platter. Serve accompanied with the bowl of mustard butter.

Rambunctious Riblets

SERVES 8 TO 10, THREE OR FOUR RIBS EACH

These Caribbean-style ribs are rather sticky, yes, but that's never a problem for Southerners. We don't need bibs with our seafood, thank you, and we shan't worry about a lil' sauce on our shirts. (It's often a badge of honor.) You'll need 2 to 4 cups apple or pecan wood chips to get a slightly sweet, smoky flavor, but hickory's another good bet.

4 pounds lean pork baby-back ribs

2 tablespoons olive oil

3 tablespoons Jamaican jerk rub

Two 12-ounce cans root beer

Zest and juice of 2 oranges

1 cup rum or bourbon

1 cup sugar

¼ cup hot-pepper jelly

¼ cup steak sauce

2 teaspoons Pickapeppa sauce

2 sticks cinnamon

5 whole cloves

Rub the ribs with the olive oil and sprinkle with the Jamaican jerk rub. Cover and refrigerate at least several hours, or up to 12 hours, before cooking. (Over-marinating will deepen the flavor but also break down the texture of the meat.)

Soak 2 to 4 cups wood chips or chunks in water for at least 30 minutes.

In a medium Dutch oven over high heat, bring the root beer, orange zest, orange juice, rum, sugar, hot-pepper jelly, steak sauce, Pickapeppa sauce, cinnamon, and cloves to a boil, stirring often. (Watch carefully, holding a tight-fitting lid; if the rum ignites, quickly cover the saucepan to tamp out the flame before removing the lid.)

Turn the heat to medium and cook, stirring occasionally, until the mixture reduces to a glaze consistency, 20 to 25 minutes. Remove the sauce from the heat and strain it through a fine-mesh strainer. Divide the glaze into two equal portions; set aside.

Prepare a grill by piling lava rocks or charcoal on each side, leaving a center section empty; place a drip pan underneath. (It isn't necessary, but it helps with the grill cleanup.)

Drain the soaked wood chips and place them directly over the heat source in a smoker box or on a square of heavy-duty aluminum foil that's been folded and perforated several times. Heat the grill to 350° to 400°F.

Arrange the ribs over the heat to either side of the drip pan and cook, with the grill covered, 12 to 15 minutes on each side. Baste the ribs with the glaze mixture, then remove them from direct heat, placing them over the drip pan. Cook them, covered with the lid, 5 to 6 minutes more on each side, or until the meat is tender, basting often. Serve them with the reserved glaze.

Dr Pepper Brisket & Brie Quesadillas with Peachy BBQ Sauce

SERVES 10, TWO OR THREE WEDGES EACH; MAKES 2 CUPS SAUCE

Treat guests to flavor and more flavor by way of an unexpected quartet of tender brisket, sweet peaches, creamy Brie, and a spicy, fruity barbecue sauce. This makes superb use of peaches when they're ripe and plentiful (June through August). Georgia has some good ones, but I'm smitten with the rich yellow ones grown near Ruston, Louisiana, especially the ones from Mitcham Farms, owned and operated by the same family for seventy years (see Sources, page 138).

PEACHY BBQ SAUCE

1 tablespoon canola oil

¾ cup coarsely chopped sweet onion

1 to 2 jalapeño peppers, halved and seeded

¼ teaspoon sea salt

1 pound fresh peaches, peeled and coarsely chopped

¼ cup cider vinegar

¼ cup bourbon

2½ tablespoons light honey

2 tablespoons Dijon mustard

1 tablespoon tomato paste

¼ teaspoon chili powder

1 teaspoon molasses or light brown sugar (optional)

⅛ teaspoon dry mustard (optional)

To make the BBQ sauce: In a heavy medium saucepan over medium heat, warm the canola oil and cook the onion, jalapeños, and ⅛ teaspoon of the salt, stirring occasionally, until the vegetables are soft and tender, 8 to 10 minutes.

In the bowl of a food processor, combine the cooked vegetables, peaches, cider vinegar, bourbon, honey, Dijon mustard, tomato paste, chili powder, and remaining ⅛ teaspoon salt. Purée until just blended.

Transfer the mixture back to the medium saucepan over medium heat and simmer, uncovered, for 30 minutes, stirring occasionally. Halfway through the cooking time, taste the sauce and adjust the seasonings, adding the molasses and dry mustard (if using). Let it cool slightly. (Store in an airtight container in the refrigerator for up to 3 days.)

To make the brisket: In a cup or small bowl, stir to combine the chili powder, cumin, salt, and pepper. Rub the seasoning mixture and minced garlic over the meat, adding the red pepper flakes (if using). Add half of the sliced onion to the bottom of a slow cooker. Place the brisket on top and put the remaining onion on top of and around the brisket. Slowly pour in the Dr Pepper. Cover and cook on low for 8 hours.

Continued

DR PEPPER BRISKET

1 tablespoon chili powder

2 teaspoons ground cumin

1 teaspoon sea salt

1 teaspoon ground black pepper

3 garlic cloves, minced

One 3-pound butcher-trimmed brisket

2 to 3 tablespoons red pepper flakes (optional)

1 yellow onion, sliced

3 cups Dr Pepper, preferably the Dublin Dr Pepper made with cane or imperial sugar

Ten 8-inch soft flour tortillas

10 ounces Brie, rind removed, cut into 10 long slices

1 cup diced fresh peach, plus chopped peaches for garnish

1 cup shredded Monterey Jack cheese

Olive oil for cooking

Chopped avocado and fresh cilantro for garnish (optional)

Remove the cooked brisket from the slow cooker and let it rest for 15 minutes. Slice the brisket against the grain in $\frac{1}{8}$- to $\frac{1}{4}$-inch-thick pieces. Coarsely chop 5 cups. (Leftover meat will store well, in the sauce, refrigerated in an airtight container for up to 2 days.)

Place the tortillas on a clean work surface. To one side of each tortilla, add 1 slice Brie, $\frac{1}{3}$ to $\frac{1}{2}$ cup meat, $1\frac{1}{2}$ tablespoons diced peach, and $1\frac{1}{2}$ tablespoons Monterey Jack cheese. Fold the tortilla over and set aside.

In a large pan over medium-high heat, warm 1 tablespoon olive oil. Add two or three assembled quesadillas and lightly brush the tops with olive oil. Cook them until the bottoms are lightly browned and crisp, 2 to 3 minutes; flip and cook them another 2 minutes. Repeat the process with the remaining quesadillas.

Cut the quesadillas into two or three wedges, serve with the BBQ sauce, and garnish with chopped peaches, avocado, and cilantro, if desired.

Peppered Beef Tenderloin & Rosemary-Horseradish Cream Sauce

SERVES 8; MAKES ABOUT 1½ CUPS SAUCE

Dressier evening parties are resplendent with platters of yeast rolls paired with velvety beef tenderloin and creamy horseradish sauce accented with rosemary. To make haste in cracking the peppercorns for this, put them in a plastic zip-top bag and engage the flat side of a mallet to break them into smaller pieces. Other herbs will work well in this cream sauce, but rosemary holds the most sway. Serve split soft, warm yeast rolls on the side.

ROSEMARY-HORSERADISH CREAM SAUCE

One 8-ounce container sour cream

½ cup mayonnaise

2 tablespoons prepared horse-radish (see headnote, page 35)

1½ tablespoons finely chopped fresh rosemary

Sea salt

¼ teaspoon ground black pepper (optional)

PEPPERED BEEF TENDERLOIN

2 tablespoons tricolor peppercorns, cracked

1 tablespoon sea salt

1 tablespoon brown sugar

1 teaspoon cayenne pepper

1 teaspoon paprika

One 3-pound center-cut beef tenderloin

2 tablespoons softened butter or olive oil

To make the horseradish cream sauce: In a medium bowl, whisk to combine the sour cream, mayonnaise, horseradish, rosemary, and ¼ teaspoon salt. Adjust the seasonings by adding more salt and the pepper, if desired. Cover and chill for about 1 hour.

To make the tenderloin: Preheat the oven to 475°F. Place a wire rack in a roasting pan.

In a small bowl, stir to combine the cracked peppercorns, salt, brown sugar, cayenne, and paprika.

Pat the tenderloin dry. Rub the butter over the tenderloin, then rub the spice mixture into the meat. Cover the meat loosely with aluminum foil and let it stand at room temperature for 30 minutes to help absorb the seasonings.

Remove the foil, put the tenderloin on the rack in the prepared pan, and roast it for 10 minutes. Lower the oven temperature to 425°F and cook until a thermometer inserted into the thickest area of the meat registers 130°F for medium-rare (check after 20 minutes). Remove the roasting pan from the oven and let the meat rest for 10 minutes.

Carve the roast into ¼-inch-thick slices and serve it with the horseradish cream sauce.

Crawfish Beignets with Jalapeño Tartar Sauce

SERVES 8, ABOUT THREE BEIGNETS EACH; MAKES 1¼ CUPS SAUCE

Crawfish—the "baby lobster" of the South—nestled in cushiony beignets? Sold! These savory and soft seafood puffs, named for the simple doughnut-y fare savored along the Gulf Coast, are a warm delight to embrace at cocktail time. The batter and dipping sauces can be made earlier in the day, allowing you plenty of time to plop some lovin' spoonfuls of the mix into the fryer just before the crowd arrives. Trust me—you'll be as beloved as each little fritter.

JALAPEÑO TARTAR SAUCE

1 cup mayonnaise

1 jalapeño pepper, seeded and finely chopped

2 tablespoons sweet pickle relish

1 tablespoon chopped fresh chives

1 tablespoon capers, rinsed and drained

1 teaspoon Cajun seasoning

CRAWFISH BEIGNETS

2 tablespoons olive oil

1 pound peeled crawfish tail meat

¼ cup finely chopped red bell pepper

¼ cup fresh or frozen sweet corn kernels

3½ teaspoons low-sodium Cajun seasoning

½ cup chopped green onions

1 tablespoon minced garlic

To make the tartar sauce: In a small bowl, mix the mayonnaise, chopped jalapeño, pickle relish, chives, capers, and Cajun seasoning until well blended. Cover and refrigerate the mixture for about 1 hour.

To make the beignets: In a large skillet over medium heat, warm the olive oil. Add the crawfish, bell pepper, corn, and 2 teaspoons of the Cajun seasoning. Cook for 2 minutes, stirring constantly.

Turn the heat to low and add the green onions, garlic, and remaining 1½ teaspoons Cajun seasoning. Stir to mix evenly and cook for 1 minute. Adjust the seasoning as desired. Remove the pan from the heat and set it aside.

In a large bowl, combine the flour, milk, eggs, and baking powder; whisk until smooth. Season with the salt and pepper.

In an electric fryer, Dutch oven, or heavy cast-iron skillet, add peanut oil to a depth of 2 to 4 inches. Heat to 360°F. (If not using an electric fryer, use a fry/candy thermometer to ensure the temperature stays consistent.) Line a plate with paper towels.

3½ cups all-purpose flour

1½ cups milk

2 eggs

2 teaspoons baking powder

1 teaspoon coarsely ground sea salt

1 teaspoon ground black pepper

Peanut or vegetable oil for frying

Fresh jalapeño pepper slices and
fresh chives for garnish (optional)

Gently drop five or six heaping tablespoons of crawfish batter into the hot oil, being careful not to crowd them so they'll cook evenly. Fry for 5 to 7 minutes, turning occasionally, until the crawfish beignets are golden and cooked through. Drain on the prepared plate. Repeat until all the batter is used.

Serve the beignets immediately with the tartar sauce. Garnish with jalapeño slices and chives, if desired.

Marinated Shrimp, Tomato & Mozzarella Salad

SERVES 8 TO 10

This "wow" salad, which looks splendid in a large trifle dish, is the darling of any casual or elegant buffet-style brunch, late-afternoon gathering on the porch, or early evening cocktail party. Using packaged dressing mix keeps this super easy to make, while the white balsamic vinegar lends flavor sophistication. Bocconcini are 1- to 2-inch balls of mozzarella packed in water and found in the deli area of most large supermarkets. Serve atop a bed of butter lettuce leaves or in avocado halves, if desired.

½ cup extra-virgin olive oil

½ cup white balsamic vinegar

Two 0.75-ounce packets garlic and herb dressing mix (such as Good Seasons)

2 pounds large (21/25 count) cooked shrimp, peeled, deveined, tails removed

1½ to 2 pounds baby mozzarella balls (*bocconcini*) or cubes, patted dry

2 cups cherry tomatoes, halved

⅓ cup fresh basil chiffonade, plus more for garnish

¼ cup finely chopped green onions

In a large glass measuring cup with a spout, whisk to combine the olive oil, vinegar, and dressing mix.

In a large bowl, combine the shrimp, mozzarella, tomatoes, basil, and green onions. Pour in the dressing and use a rubber spatula to gently incorporate the ingredients. Transfer the mixture to a large plastic zip-top bag (which allows for easier shaking of ingredients, transport if taking the food elsewhere, and cleanup) and refrigerate for at least 4 but no longer than 8 hours (long marinade times compromise the shrimps' texture), shaking the ingredients occasionally to evenly marinate them.

Serve cold or at room temperature, garnished with basil.

Ooh-la-la

The French word *chiffonade* (shihf-uh-NAHD or shihf-un-NAYD) is a fancy term for cutting leafy herbs (basil, mint, sage) into super-thin and elegant ribbon-like strips. Stack seven or eight clean leaves, from largest on the outside to the smallest on the inside. Roll them tightly lengthwise, stems facing down, cigar-style. Aim a chef's knife at a 60-degree angle to carefully cut $\frac{1}{16}$- to $\frac{1}{8}$-inch-thick slices. Fluff the herb ribbons with your fingers before sprinkling atop your dish.

Pascal's Manale BBQ Shrimp

SERVES 4

The Manale family opened the eponymous New Orleans seafood restaurant in 1913. After Frank Manale's death in 1937, the place would be owned by cousin Pascal Radosta, who'd worked with Frank for decades. "The Manale," as it became known, is in its fourth generation of ownership. The restaurant's famous buttery, garlicky, peppery BBQ shrimp came onto the scene in the 1950s—apparently inspired by a dish Pascal's friend had enjoyed in Chicago. Eager to re-create it, Pascal put a Louisiana spin on it. His friend was blown away. So was the public, which sometimes waits up to two hours for it. Use head-on shrimp and your sauce will have more rich shrimp flavor.

MANALE SPICE MIX

¼ cup ground black pepper

1 teaspoon paprika

1 teaspoon salt

1 teaspoon dried thyme

1 teaspoon dried oregano

1 teaspoon dried basil

¼ teaspoon cayenne pepper

1 pound large (21/25 count) shrimp, heads on or removed

½ teaspoon minced garlic

½ teaspoon Worcestershire sauce

¼ teaspoon Louisiana hot sauce

¾ cup extra-virgin olive oil

½ cup white wine

1 tablespoon unsalted butter

Toasted French bread and lemon wedges for serving

To make the spice mix: In a small bowl, combine all the ingredients thoroughly. Store in a dry, airtight container at room temperature for up to 2 weeks.

Wash the shrimp and pat dry (being careful not to remove the heads if planning to cook them with the shrimp).

In a large nonstick skillet over high heat, combine the shrimp, spice mix, garlic, Worcestershire, and hot sauce and stir for 1 minute. (This pre-oil technique helps crisp the shrimp while adhering the seasonings.) Pour the olive oil over the shrimp, then add the white wine. Stir to blend all the ingredients thoroughly and cook for 4 minutes, stirring often (but carefully to keep the shrimp heads on, if using).

Lower the heat to medium and cook for 4 minutes more. Add the butter and cook for an additional 2 minutes, until the butter is thoroughly melted and blended in. (Add more butter if desired so it stays properly saturated. Just be careful not to overcook the shrimp or they will become tough.) Serve the shrimp in individual casserole dishes or bowls and offer toasted French bread for dipping in the sauce and lemon wedges for squeezing.

Dickie Brennan's Oyster Pan Roast

SERVES 4

In my mind, the name Dickie Brennan—or just about any Brennan, for that matter—connotes comfort food. (This is a New Orleans family who can cook, folks.) After enjoying these divine, silky, creamy, cheesy oysters one evening at Palace Café, I was hooked. Another good excuse to make this: Why not get those oyster plates you might have hanging on the wall and actually use them? This would be well worth it.

¼ cup fine, dry bread crumbs

2 tablespoons freshly grated Parmesan cheese

1 tablespoon butter, softened

Four 2-inch slices French bread

¼ teaspoon salt

⅛ teaspoon ground black pepper

2 cups heavy whipping cream

1 small shallot, chopped

1 tablespoon chopped fresh rosemary, plus 4 fresh rosemary sprigs

⅛ teaspoon ground white pepper

20 "select" (high-quality) oysters, shucked and drained

Chopped fresh Italian flat-leaf parsley for garnish

Preheat the oven to 350°F.

In a small bowl, combine the bread crumbs and Parmesan cheese; set aside.

Spread the butter on one side of each bread slice. Combine $\frac{1}{8}$ teaspoon of the salt and the black pepper and sprinkle over the butter. Place the bread slices, buttered-side up, on a baking sheet. Bake for 15 minutes, or until lightly browned and crisp. Set aside (or cover and store in an airtight container for up to 2 days).

Preheat the broiler.

In a large ovenproof skillet over medium-high heat, stir to combine the cream and shallot and bring to a boil, stirring often. Cook until reduced to 1 cup (about 15 minutes), stirring often. Stir in the remaining $\frac{1}{8}$ teaspoon salt, the chopped rosemary, and white pepper. Add the oysters and cook until the edges of the oysters begin to curl, about 1 minute. Remove the skillet from the heat. (Cut any large oysters in half or into thirds.) Sprinkle the oyster mixture with the bread crumb mixture. Broil the oysters 3 inches from the heat until the bread crumbs are golden brown, 2 to 3 minutes.

Spear a rosemary sprig through each toasted bread slice; place an herbed bread slice in each of four individual shallow bowls. Spoon the oyster mixture around the bread. Garnish with chopped parsley and serve immediately.

CHAPTER FIVE

LIQUID ASSETS:
Cocktails and Beverages

....

Spirited gatherings call for equally spirited drinks that can make the world (and your cheeks) a little rosier.

Swishy sips are expected at a proper party, not only because they make people feel special, but also because they encourage people to relax and "drop the mask," as the late, great Southern bon vivant writer Eugene Walter liked to say. I'll always cherish the warm afternoon we once spent in his Mobile, Alabama, home, sipping sherry from small jelly jars served from an antique silver tray. What brilliance, pure and simple.

The mix of liquid refreshers in this chapter ranges from crowd-size beverages intended for lovely self-serve containers and pitchers to do-it-yourself drinks that add to a party's entertainment.

All the drinks here are cocktails, but many can be made without alcohol by substituting fresh or sparkling fruit juice. Pair these elixirs with beer, wine, sparkling waters, and sodas and prove you know how to pour on the Southern charm.

Pimm's Cup, Please

The Pimm's Cup, made with herbaceous gin-based Pimm's liqueur and complete with crisp English cucumber wedge stirrer, is one posh libation. It holds a top spot in Southern cocktail aristocracy.

¾ to 1 cup Pimm's No. 1 liqueur (see Sources, page 138)

2 cups ginger ale or lemon-lime soda

Ice cubes

English cucumber slices or wedges and lemon wheels for garnish (optional)

In a cocktail pitcher, stir to combine the Pimm's liqueur and ginger ale.

Pour the mixture in cocktail glasses filled with ice and garnish with cucumber and lemon, if desired, before serving.

Gin Yummies

SERVES 4

When subtle, elegant elderflower liqueur pairs with bespoke gin, you get an elixir par excellence. St-Germain's curvaceous bottle, evoking the Belle Époque era, is one of the most beautiful on the planet. It will forever hold a place on our bar, since it adds an easy grace note to sparkling wine, lending accents of pear and citrus. Large cocktail shakers let you make four or more drinks at a time—even more if additional shakers are on the scene.

¾ to 1 cup gin

½ cup St-Germain elderflower liqueur (see Sources, page 138)

2 lemons, halved, plus lemon twists or small, thinly sliced wedges for garnish (optional)

Ice cubes

In a large (at least 24-ounce) cocktail shaker, combine the gin and elderflower liqueur. Squeeze the juice from the lemon halves into the shaker and, if desired, drop in the squeezed fruit sections. Add ice to fill and shake well.

Strain the drinks into martini glasses and garnish with the lemon twists, if desired, before serving.

Strawberry-Basil Margaritas

SERVES 4

When fresh, sweet basil meets juicy strawberries, then mingles with tequila and orange liqueur, it's nothing short of divine.

2 cups hulled, ripe, fresh strawberries

⅔ cup good tequila

3 to 4 tablespoons freshly squeezed lime juice

2 tablespoons orange-flavored liqueur (e.g., Cointreau, triple sec)

8 to 12 large fresh basil leaves, plus basil sprigs for garnish (optional)

2 to 4 tablespoons superfine sugar

Ice cubes

In a blender, purée the strawberries, tequila, lime juice, orange-flavored liqueur, and basil leaves on low speed until smooth. Taste and add your desired amount of superfine sugar. Add two handfuls of ice and purée until the ice is crushed, 30 seconds to 1 minute.

Divide the drink among four margarita glasses and garnish with basil sprigs, if desired, before serving.

Peach-Berry Sangria

SERVES 6 TO 8

Beverage dispensers are brilliant. They provide a sculptural but functional focal point for a hydration station. They let guests help themselves, which in turn leaves the party host with one less thing to worry about. And they clearly show off the beauty of the drink within— in this case, a golden sangria with an effervescent Moscato wine to bring out the fruits' rich depth of flavor. Peach nectar from concentrate can be found in the Latino food section of a supermarket.

Two 1-liter bottles peach-flavored or plain seltzer water or club soda

One 750-milliliter bottle good-quality Moscato or Riesling

Two 11.3-ounce cans peach nectar from concentrate

8 ripe peaches, sliced

4 cups fresh raspberries

8 cups ice

In a gallon-size pitcher, combine the seltzer, Moscato, and peach nectar. Cover and refrigerate for 4 hours to let the flavors coalesce.

Add about 3 cups of the peach slices and 3 cups of the raspberries (or all the fruit if not garnishing) to a beverage dispenser at least 2 gallons in size. (You also could use two 1-gallon-size pitchers.) Slowly pour the chilled wine-nectar mixture on top of the fruit, stirring gently with a long-handled wooden spoon in order to not damage the delicate fruit. Add the ice to fill the beverage dispenser. (If using pitchers, keep them cold.)

Thread the reserved peach slices and raspberries onto small wooden skewers for garnish, if desired.

Pour the sangria into cocktail glasses filled with ice and garnish with the skewers just before serving.

Stanley's Juleps with Honeydew-Mint Sorbet

SERVES 8

Juleps are traditionally made one by one, but this recipe, shared by the great food writer/ editor Stanley Dry of New Iberia, Louisiana, makes enough for a crowd. It's best served very cold—preferably with crushed or cracked ice. (If neither is available, do as my mother did: Fill a pillow case with ice cubes, set it on the kitchen counter, and use the flat end of a meat mallet to beat the living daylights out of it.) It's also advised to serve the drinks in pewter or silver julep cups, which helps keep them frosty. (Tip: Hold the cup by the base or top rim to avoid warming the drink by removing the frost that will form around the cup.) The refreshing (and, mind you, strong) drink is taken to new heights of pleasure with this heavenly sorbet.

2 cups water

¾ cup sugar

3 cups loosely packed fresh spearmint leaves, plus sprigs for garnish (optional)

2 cups bourbon

Crushed or cracked ice

8 small scoops Honeydew-Mint Sorbet (page 128)

In a medium saucepan over medium heat, stir to combine the water and sugar until the sugar dissolves. Add the mint leaves and bring to a boil. Remove from the heat, cover, and let steep for about 30 minutes.

Strain the mint syrup through a fine-mesh sieve or coffee filter and let cool. Combine with the bourbon in a sealable container. Chill for 1 hour.

Pour the bourbon-syrup mixture into julep or cocktail glasses filled with ice. Serve each drink with a scoop of sorbet and garnish with a mint sprig, if desired.

Prescription for Happiness

The first mention of juleps in print was in 1803, when an Englishman noted Virginians' fondness for morning health tonics made with mint and spirits (more than likely brandy, rum, or gin; bourbon was just being dreamed up).

To make a julep the traditional way, combine 6 or 7 mint leaves, 2 ounces bourbon, and 1 tablespoon simple syrup or superfine sugar in a pewter or silver julep cup. Use the back of a spoon to gently crush the mint and release its essence into the liquid. Fill the cup with crushed or cracked ice. Gently press the spoon into the ice, shaking it to incorporate the bourbon-syrup mixture.

Honeydew-Mint Sorbet

½ cup superfine or granulated sugar

½ cup water

8 to 12 fresh spearmint leaves

4 cups honeydew melon cubes, frozen

Juice from ½ lime

In a small saucepan over medium heat, stir to combine the sugar and water. Stir often to ensure the sugar thoroughly dissolves while the mixture heats to a boil. Remove from the heat and stir in the mint leaves. Cover and let the mixture steep as it cools. Strain the room-temperature syrup into a clean container. (Store, covered, in the refrigerator for up to 1 month.)

In the bowl of a food processor, purée the frozen melon, minted syrup, and lime juice until the mixture is creamy (but not liquefied), scraping down the bowl sides as necessary to evenly blend. Remove the sorbet mixture to an airtight container and freeze until firm, about 4 hours. (If the sorbet gets too hard to scoop, let it sit at room temperature about 15 minutes to soften.) Store in an airtight container in the freezer for up to 1 month.

Apple Brandy Dandies

SERVES 6

Birds of a feather flock together—in this case, distilled wine brandy with Prosecco, a sparkling cousin. Apple brandy's been a Southern favorite for ages, and homegrown varieties, like Carriage House Apple Brandy from Carolina Distillery in North Carolina or the one from Georgia's Ivy Mountain Distillery (see Sources, page 138), can help you get that authentic Southern fall spirit. This also will work with other flavored brandies, though.

6 sugar cubes

6 tablespoons apple brandy

One 750-milliliter bottle Prosecco, chilled

Thin apple slices for garnish (optional)

Put a sugar cube in each base of six champagne flutes. Add 1 tablespoon apple brandy to each flute. Top off with the Prosecco and perch an apple slice on the side of each glass, if desired, before serving.

Honeysuckle-Watermelon Refreshers

SERVES 8

This beguiling cooler is liquid bliss. Refreshingly crisp watermelon is made exceptional with honeysuckle vodka from Mississippi distillery Cathead Vodka (see Sources, page 138), but just about any citrusy vodka would make this a fine drink. The distillery, whose name pays homage to the South's cool blues "cats," is dedicated to supporting Southern tastes and traditions through its products (they also make a pecan vodka) and philanthropic work (they support Southern blues musicians, folk artists, and writers). I'll drink to that.

8 cups seeded, cubed watermelon, plus wedges for garnish (optional)

2 cups lemon-lime soda

1 to 1½ cups honeysuckle vodka

¼ cup freshly squeezed lime juice

¼ cup light honey, agave nectar, or superfine sugar

½ cup orange-flavored liqueur (optional)

Ice cubes

Mint sprigs and lime slices for garnish (optional)

In a blender or food processor, purée the watermelon cubes until smooth. Strain the watermelon pulp through a fine-mesh strainer into a large pitcher, using a spoon to squeeze out as much juice as you can. Discard the remaining pulp.

Stir in the lemon-lime soda, vodka, lime juice, honey, and orange liqueur (if using). Stir gently and pour the drink into cocktail glasses filled with ice. Garnish with watermelon wedges, lime slices, and mint sprigs, if desired, before serving.

Pitcher-Perfect Mimosas

SERVES 10 TO 12 (WITH REFILLS)

This go-to sparkler offers just the right refreshing citrus flavor—not too sweet, not too woozy-ing. The personalization possibilities are endless, including substituting pineapple juice concentrate and/or one of the many fruit-flavored sparkling juices now on the market.

12 ounces frozen orange juice concentrate, thawed

2 ounces frozen limeade concentrate, thawed

2 cups cold water

6 cups cold sparkling wine (like Prosecco) or sparkling apple or white grape juice

Berry Nice Ice (optional)

In a large container, combine the orange juice concentrate, limeade concentrate, and water. Cover and chill for 2 to 24 hours.

Divide the orange juice mixture among two large pitchers and refrigerate for another 2 hours. Just before serving, carefully add the sparkling wine.

Pour the mimosas into cocktail glasses filled with Berry Nice Ice, if desired, and serve.

Berry Nice Ice
* * *

Here's a nifty way to jazz up most any of the beverages in this chapter. Fill two ice-cube trays with small fresh strawberries, blueberries, or raspberries. Add white grape juice or distilled water (to avoid cloudy ice) and freeze.

Comfort 'n' Sweet Tea

MAKES 2½ QUARTS; ENOUGH FOR 40 COCKTAILS

I often joke that sweet tea is in Southerners' DNA, but there is some truth to that. The region's earliest party hosts, after all, were descended from English, Scottish, and Irish tea fanciers who countered the South's sultry climate by serving the traditionally hot beverage on ice. Then came the sugar (lots of it, apparently), as it was accessible and abundant, a recognized preservative and a certified energy-enhancer. Here, it's at the heart of a sprightly elixir that can be served casually from an agua fresca *container or vintage pickle jar alongside a ladle and passel of canning-jar glassware. For fancier parties, use a pretty pitcher to pour the well-chilled drink into martini glasses.*

· · ·

10 cups water

2 family-size or
8 regular black tea bags

¾ cup sugar

7½ cups Southern Comfort liqueur

5 cups sour mix

Ice cubes (optional)

Lemon slices and mint sprigs
for garnish (optional)

In a large saucepan over high heat, boil 3 cups of the water. Add the tea bags and continue boiling for 1 minute. Remove from the heat, cover, and steep for about 15 minutes. Remove and discard the tea bags. Add the sugar, stirring to dissolve. Pour the tea mixture into a 1-gallon container, then add the remaining 7 cups water. Add the Southern Comfort and sour mix. Stir to combine and refrigerate until chilled. (Serve within 1 day to keep the flavors at their brightest.)

Pour into chilled martini glasses or over ice in cocktail glasses and garnish with a lemon slice and mint sprig, if desired, to serve.

What a Comfort

· · ·

Southern Comfort isn't whiskey; it's a liqueur made with a secret formula of fruit and spices to give it a whiskey flavor. It was created in New Orleans in 1874 by Irish-born bartender Martin Wilkes Heron, labeled by some cocktail historians as America's "original mixologist."

DIY BLOODY MARYS

A well-seasoned Bloody Mary is the quintessential brunch drink. And football-watching drink. And sunset-watching drink. And sunrise-watching drink. Okay, so it's an anytime drink, really. Since everyone likes their Bloody Marys just so, why not have a DIY station with an array of flavor boosters for guests to create their own singular sensation?

Keep the mixture cold by tucking a pitcher in ice or serving it in a drink dispenser with an ice insert. (That'll help keep the ice from melting once you add vodka to the drink.) I enlist a vintage plant stand to display a "Bloody Mary Bar" sign as well as a variety of flavor boosters to accompany a pitcher or two of pre-made Bloody Mary Base (facing page) that just needs your own personal touch. Don't let all the items you see here stress you out; just pick your favorite options. Employ a console table as a makeshift bar where one or two easy-to-clean cutting boards can serve as bases for people to stir and garnish their drinks as desired.

Flavor Boosters

- Vodka, regular or flavored (e.g., citrus or pepper)
- Prepared horseradish (see headnote, page 35)
- Worcestershire sauce
- Freshly squeezed lime juice and/or lemon juice
- Sea salt
- Ground black pepper
- Mild hot sauce
- Clam juice
- Garlic salt/powder
- Ground cumin
- Celery salt

Garnishes

- Cajun or Old Bay seasoning (for rim of glass and/or drink seasoning)
- Celery ribs (preferably with leaves)
- Fresh sprigs of rosemary, cilantro, basil, and/or parsley
- Lemon and/or lime wedges
- Pickled okra and/or green beans
- Pepperoncini
- Carrot sticks
- Cherry tomatoes on skewers
- Pimiento-stuffed olives on skewers
- Gherkins on skewers
- Fresh cucumber wheels or wedges
- Peeled, chilled boiled tail-on shrimp, or blue crab claws
- Fried pork rinds

Bloody Mary Base

SERVES 10 TO 12; MAKES 8½ CUPS

This recipe is a good starter on which to build the flavors of a Bloody Mary. Use my suggestions for flavor boosters and garnishes or see the Cooking Note for a great-tasting version that works for me every time.

8 cups tomato juice

¼ cup prepared horseradish (see headnote, page 35)

¼ cup Worcestershire sauce

In a large pitcher or drink dispenser, combine the tomato juice, horseradish, and Worcestershire. Store in the refrigerator for up to 1 week.

Cooking Note

To make a fully prepared batch of my favorite version of Bloody Marys, prepare the Bloody Mary Base in a gallon-size pitcher. Add 2 cups vodka, ¾ cup freshly squeezed lime juice, 1 tablespoon hot sauce, 1 tablespoon horseradish, 1 tablespoon Worcestershire, 1 teaspoon sea salt, 1 teaspoon ground black pepper, and 1 teaspoon Cajun or Old Bay seasoning. Stir to combine and refrigerate until cold.

Party Themes & Menus

So many choices! When planning your next party, consider these seasonal party themes and a smattering of fitting fare within this book.

New Year's Day Celebration

Fried Black-Eyed Peas (page 25)

Creamy Collard Greens Spread (page 62)

Shrimp Butter (page 74) with Toasted Crostini (page 81)

Lil' Natchitoches Meat Pies (page 44) with Goodly Ranch Dip (page 58)

Rambunctious Riblets (page 104)

DIY Bloody Marys (page 134)

Mardi Gras/Jazz Brunch

Muffaletta Bites (page 28)

Oysters Rockefeller Spinach Dip (page 60)

Shrimp & Gritlets with Emeril's Tomato Jam (page 30)

Crawfish Beignets with Jalapeño Tartar Sauce (page 110)

Dickie Brennan's Oyster Pan Roast (page 116)

Pascal's Manale BBQ Shrimp (page 115)

Stanley's Juleps with Honeydew-Mint Sorbet (page 126)

Bridal/Graduation Shower

Fanciful Cheese Straws (page 20)

Cornbread Blinis (page 83) with smoked salmon and Lemon Aioli (see page 92)

Curried Chicken Salad (page 49) in mini tarts or finger sandwiches

Brandied Baked Ham with Mustard Butter (page 102) and biscuits

Marinated Shrimp, Tomato & Mozzarella Salad (page 112)

Pitcher-Perfect Mimosas (page 132) or sparkling fruit juice

Afternoon Garden Party

Best Pimiento Cheese (page 52) on cucumber slices

Tomato Aspic (page 86)

Spinach Salad with Strawberries, Bacon, Blue Cheese & Bourbon Vinaigrette (page 89)

Minted Watermelon & Feta Salad (page 88)

Fresh Corn Cakes with Field Pea Relish & Lemon Aioli (page 92)

Herbed Goat Cheese & Tomato Tarts (page 95)

Pimm's Cup, Please (page 120)

Summer Shindig/Porch Party

Lima Bean Hummus (page 68)

Strawberry-Beet Salsa (page 73) with Sweet Potato Crisps (page 78)

Buttermilk-Battered Okra Fries with Comeback Sauce (page 36)

Wee Chicken & Waffles with Jezebel-Maple Syrup (page 35)

Honeysuckle-Watermelon Refreshers (page 131)

Peach-Berry Sangria (page 125)

Cinco de Mayo Fiesta

Chunky Guacamole (page 70) with Sweet Potato Crisps (page 78)

Roasted Tomato Salsa (page 71) and Queso Fundido, My Darling (page 57) with Homemade Tortilla Chips (page 80)

Tequila-Spiked Cocktail Sauce with Perfectly Boiled Shrimp (page 77)

Dr Pepper Brisket & Brie Quesadillas with Peachy BBQ Sauce (page 105)

Strawberry-Basil Margaritas (page 123)

Tailgate/Casual Fall Gathering

Corndog Pups with Honey of a Mustard Sauce (page 42)

Debonaire Deviled Eggs (page 26; use sliced chives for football "laces")

Jars o' Cornbread Salad (page 91)

Chicken Tortilla Soup (page 98)

Fried Catfish Po' Babies with Creole Rémoulade Sauce (page 39)

Rum 'n' Coke Wings (page 100)

Comfort 'n' Sweet Tea (page 133)

Elegant Fall/Holiday Fête

Bourbony Chicken Liver Pâté (page 66)

Charleston Cheese Ball (page 55)

Divine Crab Spread (page 65)

Oysters Rockefeller Spinach Dip (page 60)

Rhapsody in Blue, Fig & Rustic Ham (page 32)

Peppered Beef Tenderloin & Rosemary-Horseradish Cream Sauce (page 109) with yeast rolls

Apple Brandy Dandies (page 129)

Gin Yummies (page 122)

Sources

Adobo with cumin seasoning
Goya.com/201-348-4900

Apple brandy
Carolinadistillery.com/828-499-3095
Ivymountaindistillery.com/706-778-5550

Aspic six-cavity silicone mold: "Blossom" by Freshware
Amazon.com and other online sellers

Baby beets, peeled, steamed (8-ounce packages)
Melissas.com/800-588-0151
Traderjoes.com

Boscoli Family Italian Olive Salad
Boscoli.com/504-469-5500

Cavender's Greek Seasoning
Greekseasoning.com/870-741-2848

Dalmatia Fig Spread
Dalmatiaimports.com/305-394-9500

Emeril's Essence
Emerils.com/504-524-4241

Honeysuckle Vodka, Cathead Distillery
Catheadvodka.com/601-667-3038

Liqueurs
Herbsaint: Sazerac.com/866-729-3722
Pernod: Pernod-ricard-usa.com/630-574-3800
Pimm's: Anyoneforpimms.com/0845-862-5652
St-Germain: Stgermain.fr/855-326-4746

Ruston, Louisiana, peaches; shipping late May through August (dates vary)
Mitchamfarms.com/318-255-3409

Stone-ground cornmeal
Anson Mills, Ansonmills.com/803-467-4122

Tony Chachere's Creole Seasoning
Shop.tonychachere.com/800-551-9066

Zatarain's Seafood Seasoning and Zatarain's Concentrated Shrimp & Crab Boil
McCormick.com/800-632-5847

Acknowledgments

To our literary agent, Angela Miller, for seeing the possibilities and believing in our abilities.

To Amy Treadwell, for making good books grand. And to Doug Ogan, Alice Chau, Tera Killip, Amy Cleary, Ann Rolke, and the rest of the Chronicle Books team, for producing some of the coolest, quirkiest books on the planet.

To Dempse and Anne McMullen and Nathalie Meurthe, for sharing their love and talent to help make us look good.

To our neighbor, Katherine Heidt, for lending us her wonderful Winnetka Heights porch.

To the Historic Natchez Foundation in Mississippi for the lovely vintage wallpaper pattern that adorns the cover of our book.

Index

Table of Equivalents

The exact equivalents in the following tables have been rounded for convenience.

Liquid/Dry Measurements

U.S.	Metric
1/4 teaspoon	1.25 milliliters
1/2 teaspoon	2.5 milliliters
1 teaspoon	5 milliliters
1 tablespoon (3 teaspoons)	15 milliliters
1 fluid ounce (2 tablespoons)	30 milliliters
1/4 cup	60 milliliters
1/3 cup	80 milliliters
1/2 cup	120 milliliters
1 cup	240 milliliters
1 pint (2 cups)	480 milliliters
1 quart (4 cups; 32 ounces)	960 milliliters
1 gallon (4 quarts)	3.84 liters
1 ounce (by weight)	28 grams
1 pound	448 grams
2.2 pounds	1 kilogram

Lengths

U.S.	Metric
1/8 inch	3 millimeters
1/4 inch	6 millimeters
1/2 inch	12 millimeters
1 inch	2.5 centimeters

Oven Temperature

Fahrenheit	Celsius	Gas
250	120	1/2
275	140	1
300	150	2
325	160	3
350	180	4
375	190	5
400	200	6
425	220	7
450	230	8
475	240	9
500	260	10